Joyfully Together

The Art of Building a Harmonious Community

Thich Nhat Hanh

Parallax Press

BERKELEY, CALIFORNIA

Parallax Press
P.O. Box 7355
Berkeley, CA 94707
www.parallax.org

Parallax Press is the publishing division of Unified Buddhist
Church, Inc.

Cover drawing by Nguyen Dong.
Cover and text design by Gopa & Ted2, Inc.

Library of Congress Cataloging-in-Publication Data

Nhât Hanh, Thích.
 Joyfully together : the art of building a harmonious community
/ Thich Nhat Hanh.
    p. cm.
 ISBN 1-888375-32-9 (pbk.)
 1. Religious life—Buddhism. 2. Buddhism—Doctrines. I. Title.
BQ5395 .N46 2003
294.3'378—dc21
                                    2003013953

1 2 3 4 5 / 07 06 05 04 03

∝ Contents

❧ Introduction

EVER SINCE I was a young monk, my dream has been to build a happy Sangha. Now, after sixty years of monastic practice, I continue to feel that Sangha building is the most precious work that we can do as practitioners. The Sangha is our community of practice, and it is also our refuge. We rely on it and trust it to support our deepest aspirations and to give us energy and inspiration on the path of practice.

The practices in this book are all real methods that we have used to resolve real conflicts in our own practice community of Plum Village. Each practice has arisen in response to the true needs, difficulties, and aspirations of the members of the Sangha. These practices and methods of transformation can also be applied to communities of practice, to families, to nonprofit and professional organizations, and to government entities. We all live and function within different kinds of communities, and any community or organization will benefit from the kinds of practices that will improve communication and mutual understanding and support among the members.

Many practices described here—such as Shining Light, Beginning Anew, the role of the abbot and abbess, the mentor system, the Day of Living Together as a Spiritual Family, the Sutra on Measuring and Reflecting, and the Seven Methods of Resolving Conflicts—have their roots in traditional monastic practices used in the Buddhist community for over 2,600 years. We have looked deeply into these traditional practices to understand the essence of them, and we have refreshed these practices, offering them in a new way that is more suitable and inspiring for us today.

Other practices offered in this book are innovations, not found before in Buddhist traditions but always inspired by them. These practices also came out of our looking deeply into the essential teachings of the Buddha and the real needs of our community. These practices include the Second-body System, the Caretaking Council, Sangha Eyes, Practicing with the Triangle, and family practices such as the Cake in the Refrigerator and the Breathing Room.

All of the practices and teachings in this book help us to ensure the harmony and happiness of the entire Sangha body. When there is happiness in a Sangha, that Sangha can help so many people.

Any group of people can practice as a Sangha, as a community that is determined to live in harmony and awareness. All we have to do is commit ourselves to going together in the direction of peace, joy, and freedom. Together, we benefit from each other's strengths and learn from each other's weaknesses. A family is a Sangha; the members of a monastic and lay practice center are a Sangha; even the United Nations is a Sangha! A Sangha is a family, a spiritual family connected by the practices of mindfulness, concentration, and insight. The Sangha may be Buddhist, or even non-Buddhist, so long as it is a community that walks the path of liberation together.

To fulfill this goal, we need concrete practices, we need the collective insight and wisdom to guide and support us. The Buddha needs intelligent and creative disciples to continue the tradition of understanding and love and make it fresh and vital in our modern world. Together, we can seek liberation from fear, suffering, misunderstanding, and confusion. Please be courageous in your efforts to apply these teachings to your own life for the benefit of yourself, your family, your community, and the world.

CHAPTER 1

The Power of the Sacred Forest

A SANGHA is a community of people—monks, nuns, laymen, and laywomen—who are walking together on a spiritual path. A Sangha has a great deal of strength; its members are able to protect each other, to help each other in every aspect of the practice, and to build the strength of the Sangha. We can take refuge in the Sangha in order to succeed in our practice. There are many things that are very difficult for us to do on our own, but when we live together as a Sangha, they become easy and natural. We do them without growing tired or making a strenuous effort. The Sangha has a collective energy. Without this energy, the practice of individual transformation is not easy.

We can also use the expression "Sangha body." When we live together in the Sangha it becomes a body, and each one of us is a cell in that body. If we are not part of the Sangha body, we will be isolated, hungry, and needy, and we will not have a suitable environment for practice. We can visualize the Sangha body as a forest. Each member of the Sangha is a tree standing beautifully alongside the others. Each tree has its own shape, height, and unique qualities, but all are contributing to the harmonious growth of the forest. Looking at the trees standing steadily alongside each other like that, you can sense the beauty, solidity, and power of a sacred forest.

Our Sangha body is going forward on the path of practice and its eyes are able to direct us. The eyes of the Sangha are able to see the strong points as well as the weak points of every member of the Sangha. By Sangha Eyes, we mean the insight and vision of the collective body of the Sangha, which includes the vision and insight of all of its members from the youngest to the eldest. Although the contribution of everyone's insight is necessary for the Sangha insight to be clear, it is not just a simple adding up of individual insights. The collective insight has a strength, a wisdom, and a vitality of its own, which surpasses any individual insight.

We learn how to use the eyes of the Sangha, considering them to be our own. If you know how to use the eyes of the Sangha, you will make your Sangha body stronger and healthier every day. Whenever the Sangha body praises or instructs you, please kneel down with joined palms and listen deeply to everything that is said. It is the Sangha that helps us make progress on the path of practice. If we respond with pride and egotism, we will never be able to make progress. We need to hear the truth about ourselves as others see it.

The energy of the Sangha body has the capacity to protect and transform us. As a member of the Sangha, all we have to do is to make our contribution to that energy. This is called Sangha building. It is the most precious work a monk, nun or layperson can do.

Each one of us needs to build the Sangha, because the Sangha is our place of refuge. The best way of building the Sangha is to turn ourselves into a positive element of the Sangha body by the way we walk, stand, sit, or lie down in mindfulness. When others in the Sangha can see our stability in this way, they also will become solid.

We build the Sangha by coming back to ourselves through mindful breathing, and not by finding fault with others when things do not go well. Criticizing and blaming others instead of concentrating on our own practice takes away the peace and joy of the Sangha and makes the Sangha more unsteady and unhappy. Although a Sangha may have weak points and shortcomings, it is still one of the three precious jewels—Buddha, Dharma, and Sangha—and it is a place of refuge for us. Our success or failure as practitioners and our happiness in life depend on whether we have the capacity to contribute in the practice of Sangha building.

The strength of the Sangha does not arise automatically. It is the product of the work of many individuals. The collective energy is made up of the combination of many individual energies. If you want the Sangha to be strong, solid, and full of energy, you, as an individual, have to contribute your own energy to the Sangha. When you are present with the Sangha in mindfulness, you automatically contribute more energy to the Sangha and the Sangha becomes stronger. When you are absent from Sangha activities, you are not able to contribute your living energy to the Sangha, and the Sangha does not profit from your energy.

For example, when the bell of mindfulness is invited—even if you are out in the garden or working in the kitchen—if you come back to yourself by means of mindful breathing, you are contributing to the Sangha energy and making it stronger. This is your contribution to building Sangha. You can also have confidence that your brothers and sisters in the practice, wherever they are, are also breathing mindfully and producing energy for the Sangha when they hear the sound of the bell. We support each other with our practice of mindfulness wherever we are and whatever we are doing. In this way, we feel there is no separation between us.

When the bell is invited to announce the meal, do not feel that if you linger where you are for another three or four minutes, it will not make any difference. Do not delay, thinking: The line is still very long. If I go and stand in the line, I will be wasting my time. When you hear the bell inviting you to the meal, you should put down the work you are doing in order to contribute your presence to the Sangha. Standing in line with the rest of the Sangha, you can practice breathing in mindfulness. Your presence is then a very valuable contribution to the Sangha. Thanks to your standing there, your friends will feel more solid in the practice when they step into the dining hall. Standing in line, dwelling in mindfulness, aware of your Sangha around you, you are already practicing to live together peacefully and joyfully.

Maybe you have had the experience of practicing walking meditation with a Sangha. When you practice walking meditation, with each step you take your mindfulness is able to help and support the people around you. Your presence is essential to your friends in the practice. Do not deprive them of this opportunity to profit from your energy of mindfulness. The Sangha needs your energy, and you also need the energy of the Sangha. If you do not practice together with the Sangha, you are not able to enjoy the collective energy of the Sangha and you will go hungry. Your mind of love will waste away a little bit more every day if you do not nourish it with the energy of the Sangha. Without a strong mind of love, you will not be successful in your life of practice, and you will not be able to contribute your share to building the Sangha.

The Capacity to Build Sangha

While I was growing up as a novice monk and young bhikshu, I looked around me and saw that many of the respected elders in the congregation were excellent scholars, gave very good teachings, and had the ability to build temples and form congregations, but few had the capacity to build Sangha. However, I remember two high monks as true Sangha builders. They were Upadhyaya Tri Thu at the Paramita Temple in the village of Vi Da and Upadhyaya Thien Hoa at the An Quang Temple in Saigon.[1] These two monks were like mother hens. They spread out their wings to shelter and bring up countless baby chicks, including them all in their warmth.

The Buddha Shakyamuni also knew the art of Sangha building. Even after only a few years of teaching the Dharma, he had built a Sangha of more than 1,200 monks and nuns. Only because he had a strong Sangha could the Buddha be so successful in offering the Dharma. In the discourses and the teachings on monastic discipline given by the Buddha we learn how his Sangha practiced mindfulness, compassion, and understanding. Many monks and nuns were able to realize the fruits of the path. We also learn that jealousy and attachment sometimes arose in the lives of the monks and nuns. But the presence of these profane elements in the Sangha did not diminish the value and the effectiveness of the Sangha as a whole. King Prasenajit recognized this when he said to the Buddha: "World Honored One, every time I look at the Sangha, my confidence in the Buddha becomes stronger." Today we still belong to the Sangha body of the Buddha.

To build a Sangha, we need to have the skill and know the art of Sangha building. Wanting to build a Sangha is not enough. We have to live and practice in a Sangha. We have to experience life in the Sangha, which means interacting with members of the Sangha whether that interaction is pleasant or unpleasant. This will give us enough understanding about how members of the Sangha can live together in harmony. In the Sangha body we live with people who can be very kind, peaceful, and joyful. At the same time we might also live with people who have difficulties that make them harsh and inclined to discriminate and judge. We should recognize that it is not only others who have this kind of unwholesome habit energy. We too have these seeds. If we do not practice mindfulness, then we cannot transform our habit energies to help build a happy Sangha. When we make our brothers and sisters happy, then we are nourishing our own capacity to build the Sangha.

Those of us who live in a Sangha need to emphasize the practices that are part of Sangha building. They are even more important than studying the sutras, practicing sitting meditation, listening to Dharma talks, or attending Dharma discussions. We should know what it means to be a good elder brother or sister, to create happiness in our Sangha. We must have the capacity to love our younger brothers and sisters even though they have shortcomings and difficulties, even though they may speak in a rough way to us, misunderstand us, or dislike us. We practice to forgive, embrace, understand, and love them as we do everyone else.

If we reprimand and blame, we will not be successful in building Sangha. Here is a small example from our monastic life. Suppose you see a younger monk or nun wearing colored socks and you say to them: "You're not supposed to wear colored socks. Why don't you do as your teacher has told you?" That younger brother or sister might become resentful and wear colored socks more frequently as a form of protest. The result is that something very small makes the atmosphere suffocating for the whole Sangha because you do not know how to use gentle and skillful speech.

How can we love someone who is difficult to love? The best way is to look deeply in order to see her situation clearly and the difficulties in which she is caught. When we can understand that, we automatically accept that person and feel love for her. Through understanding someone's difficulties, we are able to live happily and harmoniously, creating peace and joy for our Sangha at the same time. This is a practice that needs perseverance.

In the example, we can only help our younger sister when we know how to love her. Maybe the younger sister does not have many clean socks left, and today it's much colder than normal so she had to wear a pair of colored socks. If we do not try to understand her but just go ahead and correct her, our instructions will be unsuccessful from the very start because they are based on a wrong perception about our younger sister.

If we are an elder sister or brother, we have to act in such a way that our capacity to communicate remains solid, and the bridge of understanding is maintained between us and other members of our Sangha. When this bridge collapses, there is no help for us. There are moments when an elder brother cannot speak to his younger brother, or when a group of younger brothers cannot speak to a group of elder brothers. If no one among these brothers calls on the help of the whole Sangha body to restore the communication between them, they all fail in their way of dealing with each other.

But it is not only the responsibility of elder brothers and sisters to practice. The younger brothers and sisters also need to practice to establish communication. If we are not able to establish communication with our elder brothers and sisters, then our practice of transformation will not be successful. All we need is to practice mindfulness diligently every day to recognize what is happening in our own mind. Then we will be able to establish communication with our brothers and sisters.

Skillful Means

Our spiritual ancestors have created skillful means for us to help each other. When sweet medicine is needed, we can give sweet medicine. When bitter medicine is needed, we can give bitter medicine. When flexibility is needed, we can be flexible; when firmness is needed, we can be firm. Whatever method we use, it should always be practiced with compassion.

Compassion does not mean that we just allow someone to continue to behave in an unwholesome way. If we are not able to help our brother or sister, it is because we do not yet know how to apply skillful means. When we commit ourselves to Sangha building, we have to learn when to be gentle and when to be firm. Sometimes we have to act swiftly and not allow the situation to continue, because that is the only way to express our love.

When we visit a temple in Asia, we generally see two statues in the corner of the entryway. One is the gentle man and one is the fierce man. The gentle man has a very kind face and is holding a lotus in his hand. The fierce man has a cruel face and is holding a weapon in his hand. We need both the gentle man and the fierce man to build the Sangha. When we study deeply the teachings of the Buddha, we know that the gentle man and the fierce man are both manifestation bodies of the bodhisattva of compassion, Avalokitesvara. The gentle man is always smiling, praising us for doing well, saying: "It's okay, don't be afraid." The fierce man is warning us: "Do not act in that confused way; if you do you will be reprimanded!" Nevertheless, the fierce man is also a manifestation of the gentle man. His heart is full of compassion, even though we may be very afraid of his appearance.

When we can see that the gentle man and the fierce man are both using skillful means, then we are able to see the true face of Avalokitesvara. We should not think that Avalokitesvara always appears gentle and loving—that whatever we do or say is okay or that she will accept everything. Avalokitesvara has much greater compassion and much greater wisdom. If we are a teacher or an elder brother or sister, we have to learn these qualities of Bodhisattva Avalokitesvara in order to help our younger siblings. We have to love without allowing our love to be misused. We have to be brave when it is time to cut and prune. This pruning may cause some pain, but that pain is only relative, just like the pain of a surgery that will eventually lead to the good health of the patient.

Loving with Equanimity

The capacity to be inclusive and embrace everyone in the Sangha body is the basic quality of a Sangha builder. There are members of the Sangha who are fresh, open, and full of goodwill. They are able to understand and receive constructive criticism. We do not need to practice much to love people who are easy to like. When we are near such people, we can just be happy in their presence. With them, the work of Sangha building is not difficult.

There will also be people who are difficult to enjoy and love. They may have prejudices, unwholesome habit energies, lack of understanding, and only a little capacity to receive criticism. We all have the tendency to want to drive out of our life the people who are difficult for us. When a member of the Sangha is very difficult, we generally say to ourselves: "We should send that person away, because he makes the whole Sangha suffer." But we need to have patience with such brothers and sisters and include them in our embrace as well. The practice of loving kindness means developing patience and an open mind. When we open our mind, we will also have room in our heart and in our home to accept those who are difficult to like, and we will not feel the need to drive them out of our life.

Inclusiveness is something we learn gradually. Inclusiveness means opening our hearts and accepting everybody, which is not always easy to do. There are some people who can open their hearts very easily to embrace all their brothers and sisters in the Sangha. There are those who have not been able to do this. They think to themselves: "Oh, there is no more room left for you in my heart." This is a natural tendency we may have.

To practice means to go in the opposite direction of this tendency. We practice to make our hearts grow more spacious every day, making it possible for us to include people we do not feel close to or do not like very much. We are the disciples of the Buddha. We cannot always do what the Buddha does, but we have taken the vow to go in that direction. This means we have to practice opening our hearts so that everyone can have a place inside.

Although this may be difficult at first, we can do it little by little. Whether we are successful or not on our path of practice depends on whether or not we are able to do this. If we just sit there picking and choosing which person to allow into our heart, then we will never be successful as a practitioner of the spiritual path. We must learn to practice equanimity, the mind that does not take sides and treats everyone equally. It is just like a mother who loves all of her children equally, whether they are easy to love or less easy to love. Some of her children have never made her suffer, but others have made her sad and been bitter towards her. As a real mother, she loves all of her children. The heart of the Buddha is like that. The Buddha does not love just a few children; the Buddha loves everyone: the human species, the animal species, the plant species, and the mineral species. Each species has a place to be freely within the heart of the Buddha.

The Buddha has taught us to love each other with the spirit of equanimity, giving everyone equal space in our hearts. It is not because that person is of the same religion or has the same color skin as we do that we love them. It is not because a person loves us that we love them. We love our brothers and sisters because they are suffering and need our love. It is as simple as that.

To practice is to learn how to love without discrimination or attachment. Maybe when a certain brother or sister is sitting next to us we feel very at ease, peaceful, and happy, so we only want to sit near that person. This may deprive us of the opportunity to be close to other brothers and sisters in the Sangha who may also need our support and our presence. If we are intelligent in our practice, although we know that sitting next to the person we love brings us happiness, we train ourselves to sit next to other people in order to understand and love them as well. In this way we will be able to go in the direction of loving without boundaries, without discrimination, and we will make progress on the path of practice.

Inclusiveness is a basic quality for someone who wants to build a Sangha, but sometimes we must also ask: how far should our inclusiveness go? The situation of the Sangha during the lifetime of the Buddha was the same. There were members of the Sangha who were very difficult, and even the Buddha had to agree sometimes to ask them to leave the Sangha. The sutras tell us about a conversation between the Buddha and a horse trainer. One day Buddha asked him: "How do you train horses? And what do you do with the difficult ones?"

The horse trainer replied: "World Honored One, with the horses who are easy to instruct I can use very gentle methods. With stubborn horses I have to use strong methods, such as the whip and spurs and other kinds of punishment. If I were to use gentle methods with such horses, the training would not succeed. There are also horses in the herd with which I need to use both the gentle method and the strong method. World Honored One, this is the way that I train my horses."

Then the Buddha asked: "If all three methods are not successful, then what do you do?"

The horse trainer answered: "In that case I have to kill the horse, because if I allowed such a horse to stay in the herd, then it would be a bad example and corrupt the whole herd of horses."

When he had finished speaking, the horse trainer looked at the Buddha and asked: "World Honored One, I would like to know how the Buddha teaches the monks and nuns, and in the case of people who are difficult to teach, what method does the Buddha use?"

The Buddha replied: "I do exactly as you do. There are monks and nuns who are very easy to teach. I need to say just a few words and speak very gently with them. There are also those who need strong methods like temporary exclusion from Sangha activities or the practice of confession and repentance.[2] There are also people who need both methods."

Then the horse trainer asked the Buddha: "World Honored Lord, if there is a case in which you are not successful in applying any of these three methods, then what do you do?"

The Buddha replied: "I do the same as you. I also kill."

"But Lord Buddha," said the horse trainer, "you practice the path of compassion; how can you kill?"

The Buddha smiled and answered: "What I mean is that we do not allow that person to stay in the Sangha anymore. If they can no longer be in the Sangha, then we say that as far as their spiritual life is concerned they have died." To become a monk or a nun is to be born into the family of the Sangha. If we are asked to leave the Sangha, this is like dying in our spiritual life.

This story reminds us that even in the original Sangha of the Buddha, there were monks and nuns who were very difficult to teach. It was not because the Buddha and the Sangha lacked love that these monks and nuns had to be excluded from the Sangha. Their presence in the Sangha did not encourage the other young monks and nuns to practice. They caused disturbance and made the Sangha unstable. In cases like this we have to be firm and ask the person to leave the Sangha. It is a last resort that we have to take to protect the Sangha.

Asking someone to leave the Sangha is not a disciplinary measure. It is a virtuous measure because it is based on loving kindness. Loving kindness is not always gentle. When a good horse trainer whips a horse, he doesn't do so out of anger; he does it to encourage the horse. It's the same in the family. When a parent can be firm with his child and he is full of compassion, he can help his child to grow up well. It was the same in the Sangha at the time of the Buddha. If a monk or a nun lived unwholesomely, the Buddha and the Sangha had no choice but to send that person away. The Buddha felt compassion and wanted to help both the Sangha and the person expelled from the Sangha. He felt no anger and had no intention to punish. He was building a Sangha out of love.

In Plum Village we have sometimes sent a monk or nun home, and we also do this out of love. We organize a farewell tea meditation for them, buy their ticket home, give them pocket money, and offer them advice so that when they return home as laypeople they will not suffer.

The Tiger Who Has Left the Mountain

When someone leaves the Sangha it will be difficult for their practice to be successful. Vietnamese people have a saying: "If the monk leaves the Sangha, the monk will be destroyed, just as if the tiger comes down from the mountain, the tiger will be caught." A practitioner may stand solid as the lord of the mountains and forests and may speak as powerfully as the tiger roars, but if he leaves the Sangha body and goes out on his own, he is just like the tiger who has left the mountain.

When we have difficulties and suffer, we have a tendency to want to run away. We long to find a place where we think life will be better for us. In your family, you might have all the material conditions you could wish for, but if you have a problem with your father, mother, brother, or sister, you will want to run away. In the Sangha, it's the same. When you are not happy with your teacher or your brothers and sisters in the Dharma, you want to run away and go somewhere else. We dream about going to a tropical island, even though we do not really know what that island might be like. In Vietnam, we dream of going to the palace of Sister Hang on the moon. Actually, the moon is unbearably cold, and there is no oxygen to breathe. All we really want to do is run away from the present moment.

When we leave our Sangha body in search of another Sangha body where we imagine we will have more peace and joy, it usually does not lead to success on our path of practice. This is because we are going in the opposite direction to the true spirit of what the Buddha taught. When we become a monk or a nun, we make the great vow: wherever we are, that place will be our place of practice. I have seen so many monks and nuns who have fallen when they left the Sangha in order to live on their own. They are like the tiger who leaves the forest.

In Plum Village, the practice of Sangha building is seen as the most important practice in our program of training. If we want to be successful in practicing and teaching the Dharma in the future, we have to learn fully how to build a Sangha right now. Someone who does not have the capacity to build the Sangha will not be able to help the world, because if we do not have the Sangha to support us, we cannot do much. A bhikshu may be very talented, but he cannot do much if he does not have the Sangha. It is most important that while you are receiving the teachings in the monastery or practice center, you learn concrete methods of Sangha building and are successful in putting them into practice.

The responsibility of any monk, nun, or layperson living in the Sangha is to stand beautifully alongside the other trees. When we stand beautifully we begin to contribute to the Sangha body, and so we are doing the work of Sangha building. We walk, stand, sit, and lie down in mindfulness. We practice mindful manners[3] and mindfulness trainings in the actions of body, speech, and mind. We put all our heart into our studies and practice. We do not go looking for little comforts, expecting this person to love us or that person to be attentive to us, growing angry when we are not treated "equally" or given our fair share. These things are not important to those on the spiritual path. The truly important thing is that we learn to stand beautifully and joyfully together with the rest of the Sangha. If we do, then quite naturally we will grow quickly, making a positive contribution to the Sangha body. This contribution will, sooner or later, bring about a great deal of happiness in the world.

CHAPTER 2

Healing Our Isolation

Forty-nine days after the Buddha realized the path of awakening, he saw that the time had come for him to return to society in order to share what he had learned and to set in motion the wheel of the Dharma. The next day, he left the village of Uruvela, said goodbye to the fresh and peaceful forest by the banks of the river Neranjara, to the bodhi tree, and to the group of children he'd met there. He took his first steps toward teaching the way of transformation to rescue beings from their suffering.

Shakyamuni Buddha's Sangha

After a day's journey, Buddha came to the Deer Park, where he met Kondañña and his four friends Bhaddiya, Vappa, Mahanama, and Assaji. There, he gave a Dharma talk on the Four Noble Truths and opened up the way of liberation for them. All five of these friends then received the bhikshu, or monk's, ordination, becoming the first members of the original Sangha of the Buddha.

Thanks to their diligent practice, these five disciples were able to come to the wonderful insight that liberated them from affliction. Kondañña, the oldest disciple in the congregation, was the first to realize the fruit of arhatship. Two weeks later, it was Vappa and Bhaddiya's turn to reach arhatship, and finally, Mahanama and Assaji realized that fruit. Buddha was very pleased. He said, "We have a community worthy of being called a Sangha, a community of people who know how to live the life of awakening."

Soon after, a young man named Yasa arrived in the Deer Park. He was longing to be able to live a wholesome life. Thanks to his good fortune, sown in the past by causes and conditions, he met the Buddha there very early one morning. The Buddha taught him the method to get in touch with all the wonderful phenomena in the universe. He also taught Yasa to recognize the true face of suffering, which comes about because of our delusion and our craving for sensual pleasures. After he heard the teachings of the Buddha, Yasa felt that refreshing drops of rain had watered his dried-up soul. He knelt down at the feet of the Buddha and asked to become his monastic disciple. The Buddha accepted. Kondañña shaved the new disciple's head and gave him a monastic robe and a bowl of his own. When a large group of Yasa's friends heard that he had become a monk, all fifty-four of them came one by one to the Buddha asking to follow him as monks. The Sangha of the Buddha had already reached sixty in number.

The Buddha received his largest number of monastic disciples one afternoon along the bank of the river Neranjara. He was discussing the primal cause of the universe and the teaching of interdependent arising with the religious leader Uruvela Kassapa, who was the teacher of a sect that worshipped fire as the source of the universe. Uruvela Kassapa was so struck by the Buddha's words that he suddenly prostrated at the Buddha's feet. Weeping, he said: "Monk Gautama, I have already wasted half of my life. Now I beg you to receive me as your disciple so that I can enjoy the good fortune to train in the path of liberation." The next day the Buddha accepted him as a disciple. When they heard the news, nearly 500 of Kassapa's disciples also asked to become monks and follow the Buddha.

Two days later, the two younger brothers of Uruvela Kassapa—Nadi Kassapa and Gaya Kassapa—brought with them their community of nearly 700 disciples and asked the Buddha if they could become monks also. In the three following months, Buddha stayed in Gayasisa to teach and train these new bhikshus. These new Sangha members were able to realize many good fruits as a result of their studies and practice. The three Kassapa brothers became skilled assistants of the Buddha in the work of guiding and teaching the Sangha.

One morning at the beginning of the rainy season, two years after the Buddha had realized enlightenment, Sariputra and Maudgalyayana met the monk Assaji as he was going on the almsround begging for food in the town of Rajagaha. They were both part of a group of wandering ascetics, and they very much admired Assaji's unhurried and liberated manner. Without hesitation, they followed him back to Suppatittha in the Palm Grove to meet his teacher. Soon, they too asked the Buddha to receive them as monastic disciples. The Buddha accepted, and in time they became two of his most outstanding disciples. When Sariputra and Maudgalyayana left their community of wandering mendicants in order to follow the Buddha, 250 others from their group joined them and asked the Buddha to accept them as disciples as well.

In this way, within a very short time after beginning teaching the path of transformation and emancipation, the Buddha had built a large Sangha. The sutras often refer to the number of the original Sangha as 1,250 bhikshus. At that time, the Buddha had not yet established the monastic discipline in the form of precepts. The bhikshus were deeply committed to the practice and in close contact with the Buddha, so there was no need for the precepts and discipline as there was later on—and still is in our time.

A Day for Living Together as a Spiritual Family

In the Buddha's day in the areas where he taught and practiced, it was the custom for other religious practitioners to meet regularly and stay together for one day in order to discuss the teachings, share about their practice, and live as a spiritual family all day long. The monks in the Buddha's Sangha asked the Buddha for permission to organize something similar. The Buddha was very open to change, and he accepted. From that time, the community of bhikshus gathered every fifteen days, living together for the whole day so that those who had just been ordained as monks could be very close to and learn from those whose virtuous qualities were already highly developed. This was a day of happiness for the whole Sangha.

This is called the *Uposatha* day in Pali or the *Upavasatha* day in Sanskrit. *Vas* means "to dwell" or "to live," and *upa* means "close". In the *Abhidharmakosasastra*,[1] Vasubandhu also teaches us that *u* means "to nourish" or "to help grow," and *tha* means "to maintain" or "to invent." In Vietnamese, we translate it as *can tru*, which means, "staying close to one another."

If we want to preserve this beautiful tradition, we should organize our Sanghas so that everyone can be present to live together for an entire day in the spirit of a spiritual family. The Uposatha day is very important to nourish the growth of our practice. This day has also become a time for the Sangha to recite the precepts together. According to the monastic tradition, we cannot fail to organize or attend the Uposatha day twice each month unless there is a serious impediment to our doing so. It is only in times of sickness, accident, fire, flood, or serious dispute in the Sangha that we have to postpone this day for reciting the precepts. We should make every possible effort to be present, from the senior members to those who have only just ordained.

This day can also be observed by laypeople together with monastics in the monastery. Already many Sanghas are practicing like this. At the Deer Park Monastery, every month the lay Sangha members gather at the monastery to recite the Five Mindfulness Trainings, the Fourteen Mindfulness Trainings, and the Two Promises for children.[2]

Everyone contributes with an offering of food to share. Everyone is welcome, including those visiting the monastery for the first time and family and friends of long-term practitioners. The atmosphere is like that of a peaceful and joyful family gathering. The children and teenagers enjoy coming and spending time together with the young monks and nuns in informal Dharma discussion, playing basketball, or learning practice songs. For adults there is also Dharma discussion on the topic of the mindfulness trainings and on how to apply mindfulness in our daily lives. The atmosphere is light and nourishing. All experience the energy and the spirit of supporting each other as members of a large family going together on the path of love and understanding.

The Elder Brothers Sariputra and Maudgalyayana

In the time of the Buddha there were many monks who played the role of wise elder brothers in the Sangha. The two eldest brothers of the Sangha were the Venerables Sariputra and Maudgalyayana. Together, they acted like the right hand of the Buddha. Both monks had to face many difficulties, usually because some were jealous of them, but they played their roles as elder brothers perfectly. The Venerable Maudgalyayana was Venerable Sariputra's good friend and the epitome of filial loyalty. That is why he is often called the Bodhisattva of Great Filial Piety. In addition, the Venerable Maudgalyayana contributed a great deal to the work of Sangha building. He practiced and transformed himself and delivered precious Dharma talks sharing his experience of the practice with his younger brothers.

The Sutra on Measuring and Reflecting

There is one exceptionally practical and valuable sutra delivered by the Venerable Maudgalyayana. It is called the *Anumana Sutra,* or the *Sutra on Measuring and Reflecting.* Even when the Buddha was alive the monks and nuns recited this sutra regularly. In the commentary on this sutra, it says that it was recited as frequently as the *Discourse on the Mindfulness Trainings.* This is proof that the Venerable Maudgalyayana's teaching was very effective in creating happiness in the daily life of the Sangha and in strengthening their practice.

This sutra is found in both the Pali and Chinese canons.[3] In the Pali canon the *Anumana Sutta* is number fifteen of the *Majjhima Nikaya.* It can be translated as the *Sutra on Inference.* The Chinese sutra is called *A Bhikshu's Invitation* or *A Bhikshu's Request.* It is sutra number eighty-nine of the *Madhyama Agama*. Its title includes the words *si liang* which mean "considering and measuring." We could also translate it as "comparing and measuring."

In this sutra we look at ourselves and we compare ourselves with a friend on the path. We observe our Dharma brother or sister and we observe ourselves, looking deeply to see the direction we should go in our practice. If there are tendencies in our brother or sister that we find unskillful, we then look at ourselves to see if we too have those tendencies. Whether we have the same unskillful tendencies more strongly or less strongly, we make the determination to practice to transform ourselves. Our own practice and transformation is the best way to help our brother or sister.

Venerable Maudgalyayana delivered the *Discourse on Measuring and Reflecting* during a rains retreat. He was sitting in the shade of a tree conversing with his younger brothers. He called more bhikshus to come so that he could instruct them. To begin, he said:

> My friends, imagine that there is a bhikshu who requests other bhikshus in saying: "My friends, please converse with me. I want you to be considerate to me and to converse with me." Why is it that one friend in the practice calls on other friends in the practice to talk to him? It is because that person fears that he is isolated in the Sangha and feels that no one in the Sangha wants to talk to him.

In the Pali version, the sutra begins:

> Friends in the practice, imagine there is a bhikshu who requests the other bhikshus by saying: "My friends in the practice, you should talk to me. I want you to be considerate to me, my friends, and to converse with me." If this bhikshu is someone whom other bhikshus find it difficult to talk to, if he is someone who has characteristics which make other people not want to talk to him, if he is

impatient, closed-minded and does not have the capacity
to receive words of criticism, advice, and instruction from
his friends who are practicing the path of purity, then the
other bhikshus will judge that they cannot talk to him,
instruct him, or have confidence in him.

From time to time there are people in the Sangha who feel isolated
and lonely. They feel that none of their brothers and sisters want to
talk to them or give them attention and that no one has confidence
in them. If we were speaking in everyday terms, we would say they
feel boycotted by the Sangha.

For comparison, let us read the beginning of the *Madhyama
Agama* version:

> My good friends, if there is a bhikshu who requests other
> bhikshus as follows: "Venerables, please talk to me, please
> instruct me, please admonish me, please do not allow me
> to fall into a difficult situation." Why should he fall into
> this difficult situation? Because, my good friends, if there is
> someone whose way of speaking is always stubborn and he
> is caught in this obstinate way of speech, his friends in the
> practice who are practicing the pure way of the path will
> not want to speak with him, they will not give him instruc-
> tion and teach him, and they will not rebuke him. Because
> of that he will fall into a difficult situation. The whole rea-
> son is his habit of obstinacy expressed in his speech.

Communication is cut off between the person and his or her
Sangha because of how he or she relates with the Sangha. Venerable
Maudgalyayana advises his younger brothers to look deeply at themselves to see whether they have negative characteristics that prevent
others in the Sangha from being close to them. This sutra is not being
addressed to just one or two people in the Sangha, but to all of us.
Anyone in the Sangha who does not practice according to this sutra

may fall into such a difficult situation. This is not because other people truly want to make our life difficult or to isolate us for some reason or other but because of our own way of interacting and behaving in the Sangha. We must look deeply to see what keeps others away from us and ask our brothers or sisters to help us. Venerable Maudgalyayana describes seventeen causes for a bhikshu to feel isolated from his Sangha, followed by seventeen virtuous qualities that cause the Sangha to respect and hold the bhikshu in affection more every day. Let us examine these.

The First Point of Reflection
*A monk is caught in unwholesome desires and is
controlled by unwholesome desires.*

The sutra continues: "In the case, my friends, that a bhikshu is caught in unwholesome desires and is controlled by unwholesome desires, his friends in the practice will find it difficult to talk to him." "Difficult to talk to" means that his friends do not have an opportunity to teach that person, to show him clearly his mistakes and to offer him guidance and support. That is why fellow monks do not have confidence in that person.

The first cause of being isolated from the Sangha is thus being caught in and controlled by unwholesome wishes. In the Chinese version of the sutra, the expression *e yu* means "evil desires." In my Vietnamese translation, I use the expression "wrong desires" to make it sound less heavy. "Evil" could also be translated as "not beneficial" or "destructive." So in English, I translate it as "unwholesome desires or wishes."

Unwholesome wishes are the kind of wishes that can destroy our bodies and our future. From time to time, we see cases where a monk or a nun is pushed by unwholesome desires, such as wanting fame, money, or sensual pleasures. But when we desire something good, then our desire cannot be called unwholesome. When our wish is to practice to transform ourselves, to bring happiness and peace to those around us, to relieve the suffering of ourselves and others, such wishes can be called wholesome wishes or desires.

"Controlled" means we are not in control of ourselves; we allow our desires to be in control. When we are dominated by our desires, we fail to see things clearly as they are, and we become stubbornly attached to our views. This stubbornness is reflected in the way we speak and in our attitude. When we are obstinately attached to our unwholesome wishes and someone else advises us to act differently, we may say: "Too bad, I'm going to do it anyway." Our Dharma sisters and brothers will make an effort to help and instruct us, but after a while they will lose their patience, growing to dislike and avoid us. If we keep speaking, thinking, and acting stubbornly, refusing to let go of our unwholesome wishes, our friends will not come and speak to us anymore. We will fall into the difficult situation of being isolated.

In the lay life, people can also be too attached to unwholesome desires. In Buddhism, we speak about the six categories of unwholesome desires: fame, wealth, sex, power, too much eating, and excessive sleep. Monks and nuns guard themselves carefully from these strong desires. Laypeople also need to look deeply to see to what extent these desires are pushing and pulling them and in what direction they truly wish to go. When we are motivated by compassion, by the desire to understand and to love, we know that we are not caught in unwholesome desires. We are not the victim of our unwholesome desires, and we do not need to suffer and to make others suffer.

When we isolate ourselves from our Dharma brothers and sisters, we gradually lose our Sangha. We may have the feeling that our Sangha has forsaken us, that this Sangha body is no longer our Sangha body. We may even think about leaving our Sangha and going somewhere else. But the real reason we feel isolated is that our own behavior in our daily life has made us unapproachable, and our brothers or sisters can no longer speak to us or teach us. Who is it that takes our Sangha away from us? We do it to ourselves. Our behaviors and our habit energies come from within our own consciousness, not from outside of us.

The Second Point of Reflection
A monk praises himself and criticizes others.

He may think that no one in the Sangha is good enough to be his elder brother or his teacher. Looking at his Dharma brothers, all he can see is their unwholesome qualities. He may not be able to see a single good quality in any of them. The truth is that he has not yet recognized the same unwholesome qualities in himself. We all have the tendency to see unwholesome qualities in others without being able to admit that we ourselves have these same qualities.

Being aware of our positive qualities can be helpful in that we can encourage ourselves to continue to cultivate what is beneficial and to be an example for others. But if we have the tendency of praising ourselves too much, we may have an unbalanced view of ourselves and not be able to see clearly our own weaknesses. At the same time, when we praise ourselves we may cut ourselves off from receiving the sincere guidance of our brothers and sisters who have had more experience in the practice than we and who can offer us advice on how to improve ourselves and how to contribute to the harmony and happiness of the Sangha.

The essence of a Sangha is a community that lives in harmony and awareness. To achieve that aim we need to rely on each other's wisdom and insight. By cultivating our humility we can gradually integrate ourselves into the Sangha body. That means allowing others to advise us, to support us, and to guide us. We are aware that we cannot grow independently from others. Our progress, our spiritual growth is interdependent with the progress and practice of the whole community. In turn we learn to offer support and guidance to others. We especially receive guidance from our elders, from those who have trodden the path before us, and we offer support to those who are younger than us. In this way there is a clear connection between everyone in the Sangha. We can also receive support from those who are younger than us, and we can offer support to our elders by our sincere and wholehearted practice.

The Third Point of Reflection
A monk is easily angered and controlled by his anger.

It is natural for us to become angry from time to time, but we should practice mindfulness when we are angry. With mindfulness we will know how to take care of our anger and not allow it to cause damage to ourselves and others. When we know how to breathe mindfully, to walk mindfully, and to look deeply into the roots of our anger, then we will no longer be mastered by our anger. On the other hand, when we are mastered by our anger, it will show clearly in our actions and our words. When we speak out of anger or act out of anger, others will withdraw from us. They will not want to approach us, and they will not want to be close to us.

Sometimes when we are angry, we do not even know that we are angry. We look at others without love and understanding, without knowing that we are looking without love and understanding. Maybe we do not know that we have an angry expression on our face or in our gestures. Maybe we say things to divide the Sangha or we bully our Dharma friends, but we do not know that our words are unkind. Instead, we think that we always speak gently and softly. Because we are not mindful, we need a mirror to show us how we really are. We can ask the Sangha to be our mirror. We can say to an elder brother: "Whenever my face gets red and I do not look or speak in a pleasant manner, then please tell me."

If someone helps us as our mirror, we will make rapid progress. When we see someone else with an angry expression on her face or we hear irritation in her voice, we will see it right away. When we meet someone else with an unkind attitude, we will feel it right away. That person is very fortunate to have brothers and sisters to remind her and to show her the times when she is not fresh and at peace. If she has Dharma friends to help her, she will be protected and be able to transform her strong habit energies.

The Fourth Point of Reflection
A monk is angry and holds a grudge.

To bear a grudge is different from being angry. Some people's anger does not last long. When it has gone, they do not think about it any more. After they have finished being angry, they can smile and talk to us in a very kind way. It is much easier to be with someone like this who does not hold a grudge for a long time afterwards.

If someone is angry but does not know how to recognize his anger, he will not be able to look deeply and transform it. His anger will be stored in the depths of his consciousness as what we call an "internal knot.⁴ This knot is what becomes a grudge or a feeling of resentment. It's like having a cold. When we become sick, if we do not take the right medicine or let someone give us a massage, our cold may go deeply into our body and become much more difficult to cure. When our anger goes deeply into our consciousness, it creates an internal knot that might cause us to have aggressive gestures or unpleasant behavior without our knowing it.

It can be dangerous when we do not have mindfulness and see what we are doing. For example, a person who is drunk will say, "Did you say I am drunk? I am not drunk." In the same way, when we hear someone say that we are angry, we will reply, "No, I am not angry." In fact, everyone else can see that we are angry. The Sangha body can be a mirror to show us our behavior. Without the mirror of the Sangha body, our spiritual life will be very difficult.

The Fifth and Sixth Points of Reflection
A monk is angry, holds a grudge, and becomes bad-tempered.
A monk is angry, holds a grudge, and speaks in a bad-tempered way.

It is not serious if someone is in a bad mood occasionally, but if he feels like this all day long, other people will find it unpleasant to be with him. They will withdraw from him, and he will feel boycotted. Our ill humor or bad temper will show itself in the gestures of the body and in the way we speak. Our words carry the vibrations of our emotions, and when we speak, others can feel our emotions. Whether we are feeling fear, despair, self-pity, or anger, they will come out in our words. Even if we are not aware of the emotion in our speech, other people will hear it clearly. It is because of our lack of mindfulness that we are not aware of our emotions. Anger can be a dangerous instrument if we do not know how to practice mindfulness and transform it. A sentence of only four words said out of anger is enough to end a good friendship; it may even cause us to lose our family or our whole community. Others may continue to greet us out of courtesy, but in actuality they do not want to have contact with us anymore.

The Seventh Point of Reflection
A monk condemns his friend in the practice who has corrected him.

A practitioner's fault may be the result of just one moment of unskillfulness or wrong perception, but because she is stubborn, she will become angry and condemn a friend who gently shows her the mistake. We condemn someone by speaking negatively of him or her. Even with our thoughts we can condemn someone; we may think: "He is not worthy to be my brother. His practice is poor, he does not love me; he does not care about me." But in fact, our friends care deeply for us, and out of this care they will show us our mistakes. Our sisters and brothers are obliged to help each other in this way. But if we are not able to listen when someone is trying to help, we are throwing away the mirror that our friend has lent us.

The Eighth Point of Reflection
A monk scorns his friend in the practice who has corrected him.

In this case, a practitioner does not want to look at his friend anymore and considers that brother who corrected him as no longer being his lifelong friend. We might think that a lifelong friend would never criticize us. In fact, a person who understands us and has enough love for us to show us our weaknesses is truly worthy to be called our lifelong friend.

When we reject our friend, we act as if we do not need him anymore, we do not appreciate his presence. That is our way of punishing him for daring to show us our mistake. That is not the best thing to do. When we push our friend away from us by ignoring him, by turning away from him we are pushing away our own opportunity to grow and to understand ourselves better. If we can practice calming ourselves and looking deeply, we will see that it is not wise to try to punish our friend in such a way. In fact we are only punishing ourselves. We are only depriving ourselves of a genuine friend. When we desert our friend like that it is as though we throw away the torch that shows us our path.

The Ninth Point of Reflection
A monk corrects in turn his friend in the practice who has corrected him.

A practitioner may say or think: "You're the person who has made that mistake, not me. You're the person who is angry and ignorant. You're the person who is unpleasant. You're the person who is bad-tempered, not me." Such a person not only fails to accept her own faults, but she criticizes the person who is trying to help her.

When a friend has the courage to offer us guidance in a gentle and skillful way, we should do our best to receive it with respect and humility. Even in the workplace we need to be able to receive the advice and guidance of our fellow workmates and our boss. If we speak back to someone who offers us advice, they will feel discouraged and may not approach us anymore. Of course, it may be that the person offering us advice does not have enough skillfulness and does not offer advice in a way that is easy for us to accept. In that case, we should practice to listen calmly and respectfully, and at a later time we can politely ask that he or she offer us advice in a way that we can receive it easily. This type of communication is very useful and can improve the atmosphere of the whole workplace.

In the family, we can practice in the same way. As mother and daughter, as husband and wife, we want to offer each other our support and help. But when we give advice, the other person may get angry, slam the door, or walk away from us, and we feel hurt. Or, when we give advice to our son or daughter, or to our mother or father, he or she responds immediately, pointing out our own weaknesses and shortcomings. This is a strong tendency in the family setting. We need to learn how to resist, how to come back to ourselves and to listen and speak with kindness, with love and respect. Not only does the son need to be able to listen and speak with respect and love to his father, but also the father should practice to listen and speak lovingly and gently to his children. In this way, the relationships in the family will blossom, and each member will have a chance to grow and to learn from each other.

The Tenth and Eleventh Points of Reflection

A monk questions in return his friend in the practice who has corrected him.
A monk evades the subject and asks irrelevant questions of the one who has corrected him.

"Questioning" is for a practitioner to repeatedly ask why his brother has corrected him. That brother will then become afraid to point out the practitioner's faults the next time. Or his questioning may have nothing to do with the matter at hand. He may change the subject, evade the correction, or show anger, and ill temper.

It is important to find the appropriate time and place to communicate. Perhaps we would like to share something with our sister or brother, with our co-worker or with our family member. First we should assess when the other person will be open to hear what we wish to say, when it is a good time to talk. If we speak at an inappropriate time, the other person may not be ready to listen. She or he will react to what we say rather than listen deeply with calmness and ease. It is both the responsibility of the person receiving the advice to practice to listen with humility and acceptance and for the one giving the advice to offer it at such a time and in such a way that it can be easily accepted.

The monk who questions in return his friend or evades the criticism will lose the opportunity to develop in his practice. A young novice who has just ordained is taught to accept all criticism by joining his or her palms and bowing, without answering back. Of course, this is not easy for everyone to do right away without some training, perhaps it is even more difficult to do outside the monastery. But when we train ourselves to see those around us as members of our own family, we will be able to go in that direction. We see that our sisters and brothers in the practice each have the potential to be our teacher. Our teacher is not only outside of us but is also present in us and in our sisters and brothers.

In the family, we can see the same thing; we can learn from our children, we can learn from our parents and grandparents. We often say that the mother and father are the children's first teachers. We learn not only from verbal guidance; we also learn from our observation of our parents, of our sisters and brothers. That is why in the spiritual family we must practice diligently to be a worthy teacher and both an elder or younger sister or brother to all the other members of our family. In this sutra, we learn to train ourselves to receive the guidance of others, and by doing so we also learn how to offer guidance skillfully.

The Twelfth Point of Reflection
A monk does not explain his behavior satisfactorily to the one who has corrected him.

This means that we are not able to explain why we did or said something that caused someone to wish to correct us. Perhaps one morning it is our turn to cook breakfast, yet we did not do so. If we could not give any explanation as to why we didn't cook breakfast, it would frustrate our sister or brother. Receiving the input of others means not only listening attentively but also sharing mindfully our side of the incident so that there can be more understanding on both sides. The one who corrects us is playing his or her part well by speaking skillfully at the appropriate time, and we in turn can play our part by listening deeply and offering an explanation of our behavior if it is helpful for the situation.

The Thirteenth Point of Reflection
A monk is unrefined and ill-willed.

"Ill-willed" in French is *de mauvaise intention,* which means that one does not have the intention to correct one's mistakes. When we do not show willingness to correct ourselves, others may lose faith in us. They may feel that their efforts are in vain and it is not worthwhile to come close to us. In a community of practice we rely on the fact that every member of the community is practicing. That is what holds us together and makes us a Sangha. Seeing the sincere efforts of our sister, we are heartened, we feel encouraged that she is also practicing to transform herself. We feel that we can rely on her. We can have faith in her and trust that she will support us, will support the Sangha with her practice and transformation. If someone is not willing to practice, is not willing to transform his shortcomings, he will exclude himself from the Sangha body.

"Unrefined" here means not to have the flavor of the practice, the flavor of mindfulness. Refinement in worldly terms may refer to one's status in society and the manners associated with wealth and power. But in the spiritual life, refinement refers to the degree of mindfulness that one has concerning the actions of body, speech, and mind. When we practice mindful manners diligently, our way of speaking, interacting with others, and moving about will appear more gentle and calm. This is an example of the kind of refinement we seek in the spiritual life.

The Fourteenth Point of Reflection
A monk is jealous and greedy.

The fourteenth reason that a practitioner becomes isolated from the Sangha is that "he is jealous and greedy." Jealousy is a common emotion, yet it can be difficult to identify. For example, we may feel aversion towards our friend in the practice. But looking deeply we do not know why we do not like that person; she is kind and warm to everyone, she is skillful at many things and always willing to help others. If she has such good qualities, why do we dislike her? When we recognize our jealousy we can smile at ourselves. We can look deeply and see that our sister has many good qualities and rather than being jealous of her it would be better if we appreciated her virtuous qualities and learned from her. In the Sangha, there may be one brother who is excellent in cooking, another talented in singing and chanting, and another brother who is skillful in Sangha building. When we recognize the positive contributions of our brothers and sisters in the community, we can feel happy that they are all there to support and nourish the Sangha body. That would be more beneficial than to feel jealous.

When we feel jealous, we lose our equanimity, and we lose our capacity to appreciate and love those around us. Instead, we can admire the good qualities of others and aspire to cultivate those qualities in ourselves. For example, when we see a sister who always walks mindfully, we can admire her capacity to walk like that and aspire to practice walking meditation everywhere we go. That is a positive feeling that can help us to progress on the path. But if, instead, when we see our sister walking mindfully, we feel resentment and aversion towards her, that will not help us or the Sangha.

To be greedy or unwilling to share is to lack generosity. We can be generous with our time, with our energy, with our skills, and with material objects. Traditionally, the mindfulness trainings speak of not stealing or not taking what does not belong to us. Being unwilling to share is also a kind of stealing. If we have more than enough bread but do not give it to someone in need, that is a lack of generosity; that is greed. The same is true when we know that other people are behind us in line, yet we take more than our share of food.

When we practice generosity in the Sangha it means that we recognize our interdependence, our interbeing nature. We are aware that what we give we will also receive. We give our love, time, and energy to others, and they also give us their love, time, and energy. Just by being present at Sangha activities we can offer our presence to the Sangha. Already that will increase the energy of the Sangha. When we come to a meal and practice looking deeply into the food, eating each mouthful in mindfulness, we are offering our practice energy to all those around us. If we withhold ourselves from the Sangha, we deprive the Sangha and deprive ourselves of being able to receive from the Sangha. That is an unfortunate situation. We will begin to feel isolated and uncared for.

In the world, we will also suffer isolation and separation from those around us if we are jealous and greedy. In the family, if one sister is jealous of the other sister, they will not enjoy being together. There will be disharmony in the family. The other members of the family might recognize this and try to intervene. The mother can try to talk to each daughter to find out what the difficulty is and find skillful ways not to water the seeds of jealousy in her children. She can help each daughter to appreciate the positive qualities in the other without comparing them to each other. This will be very helpful to maintain the happiness and joy of everyone in the family.

The Fifteenth Point of Reflection
A monk is scheming and deceitful.

When we are not honest with our brothers and sisters in the practice, they will lose faith in us and they will not trust what we say or do. We build trust in the Sangha by our willingness to practice wholeheartedly, to be present for others, and to offer our support. When our brothers and sisters see that we sincerely wish to transform our unskillfulness and to live in harmony with the Sangha, they will easily have faith in us. If, on the contrary, we hide our faults and are not honest, it will be difficult for others to come to us, to share with us, and to rely on us. We will feel isolated and alone even though we are surrounded by a Sangha body. Our own practice is the best way to keep us connected to the Sangha.

In the life of a family or in the workplace these qualities are also obstacles to our peace and happiness. For example, a group of doctors needs to be able to depend on each other, to trust each other to work successfully together. Suppose one doctor in the office is dishonest with his patients or his co-workers. This will create tension and misunderstandings among everyone in the office. Eventually, that doctor may lose his job due to his negative habits, unless a wise friend comes along to offer him support and guidance.

The workplace is a kind of family that should operate on the basis of love and understanding. When there is clear and friendly communication in the workplace, the work will flow smoothly and the workers will feel at ease with one another and able to offer their services to others more joyfully and effectively. When we notice a difficulty, we should find skillful ways to help each other. When one member of the staff knows the practice of mindfulness, she can be a light to guide others. When one member of the family is trained in deep listening and loving speech, he can share his practice with everyone in the family. Many practitioners are already doing this. There are families that have weekly meetings to practice "Beginning Anew" with each other, showing appreciation and sharing their regrets and feelings of hurt.[5] There are workplaces that practice "Shining Light" for each other, acknowledging the strengths of each worker and offering practical suggestions for improving his or her weaknesses.[6] This is the true practice of living together peacefully and joyfully.

The Sixteenth Point of Reflection
A monk is stubborn and arrogant.

When we are stubborn, we are not open to listening to others or seeing the limitations of our own way of thinking. We think our way is best and our ideas are best. We may become angry when the Sangha makes a decision that does not exactly reflect what we wanted. This is the result of our stubbornness and arrogance. We are so sure of ourselves, so sure that our view is the best. This is an obstacle to overcoming our suffering and finding peace and happiness in the present moment.

I have often said that there is no place for pride in true love. True love is a process of humility, of letting go of our individual ideas and notions to embrace and become one with another person or the Sangha body. When we are proud we can be easily wounded. We are like the tall, dry grasses that do not bend down low in the face of the winds. Instead, they try to remain standing tall and in the process are broken to pieces. Our pride is an obstacle to developing our understanding, compassion, and boundless love. When we are humble we have nothing to fear, nothing to lose. We easily flow with the circumstances that we find ourselves in and are endlessly open to learn, to practice, and to transform ourselves.

The Seventeenth Point of Reflection
A monk is attached to worldly life and finds it difficult to let go.

Even one who has become a nun may still hold on to worldly ways of behavior in her daily life. She may continue to look back fondly on her former life, speaking and acting exactly as she did before she became a nun. To become a monastic is to dedicate oneself twenty-four hours a day to the path of liberation, using all one's time and energy to pursue a life of peace, joy, and freedom. When monks and nuns become caught in worldly considerations, it is a shame for them and for everyone who is relying on them for guidance and support.

We need to practice the art of letting go to retain our liberty and our serenity. Then we can offer ourselves in many ways—to help our family members, to assist with Sangha activities, to support people in our community.

As laypeople, we can also reflect on the ways we might be caught in worldly matters. To be caught in the world means to be controlled by things like power, money, fame, and sex. When we are caught by these things, others on the spiritual path will not want to be near to us. They will shy away from us because they prefer to go in the direction of compassion, understanding, and peace. Like the lotus flower that needs the mud to grow, we need the world. But we can live in the world without being entrapped by worldly considerations. We can live with freedom and security knowing that we have a path to tread, a path of understanding and love made of concrete practices and teachings.

The Seventeen Virtuous Qualities of a Monk

Venerable Maudgalyayana taught his younger brothers that "these are the seventeen reasons that isolate a bhikshu from the rest of the Sangha, making his fellow practitioners unable to speak to him, instruct him, and show him his mistakes, until finally they will lose confidence in him." These teachings show that the Venerable Maudgalyayana was very aware of what was happening in his Sangha. It seems that today our Sangha body is not much different from the Sangha body in the time of the Buddha. We have the same problems and weaknesses as they did.

After he had spoken about the seventeen reasons that cause a bhikshu to feel isolated, the Venerable Maudgalyayana spoke about the seventeen virtuous qualities that cause the Sangha to respect and love their Dharma friends more and more every day. These wholesome qualities allow our sisters and brothers in the Sangha to approach us, teach us, and show us our faults very easily. They generate great confidence in us. These seventeen wholesome qualities are simply the absence of the seventeen unvirtuous qualities we just read about:

> My friends, for what reasons is a bhikshu seen to be one whom others can easily approach and talk to? My friends, if there is a bhikshu who is not caught in unwholesome desires and is not controlled by unwholesome desires, that virtuous quality makes it easy for his fellow practitioners to approach him and talk to him. The following are the other virtuous qualities that make it easy for fellow practitioners to approach and talk to him. He does not praise himself and criticize others. He is not angry or controlled by his anger. He does not hold on to a grudge out of anger. He is not bad-tempered because of the grudge he is holding on to. He does not say things that are bad-tempered because he does not hold a grudge. He does not condemn his brother who has shown him his mistake. He does not scorn his brother who has shown him his mistake. He does not correct in turn his brother who has shown him his mistake. He does not keep questioning his brother who has shown him his mistake. He does not evade the subject, change the subject, and ask irrelevant questions of his brother who has shown him his mistake. He does not manifest irritation and anger when he is corrected. He is able to explain his behavior to the satisfaction of the brother who has shown him his mistake. He is not unmindful and ill-willed. He is not jealous and greedy. He is not scheming and deceitful. He is not stubborn and arrogant. He is not worldly, or attached to worldly life, and he has the capacity to let go. My friends, these are the virtuous qualities that make a bhikshu someone whom others can easily approach and talk to.

Venerable Maudgalyayana continued:

> My friends, a monk needs to compare himself with other brothers in the Sangha and make the following inference: "I find a brother who has unwholesome desires and is controlled by unwholesome desires unpleasant to be with. It is difficult for me to like such a brother. In the same way, if I have unwholesome desires and I am controlled by unwholesome desires, then others will find me unpleasant to be with and will not like me."

This advice encourages us to look deeply into ourselves. We can continue looking in this way into all seventeen qualities.

Looking into a Mirror to See Ourselves Clearly

The sutra continues:

> My friends in the practice, if, when looking deeply, a practitioner sees clearly that these unwholesome states have not yet been transformed, then he must continue to practice diligently in order to transform them. If while looking deeply the practitioner sees clearly that these unwholesome states have been transformed, then he can feel joyful about this and continue to practice diligently in order to nourish and cultivate this wholesome state.
>
> My friends, imagine a young person who is fond of beautifying himself and looking at himself frequently in a clear, unclouded mirror or in a basin of clear, unclouded water. If he sees a dirty mark on his face, he will clean it right away. And if he does not see any dirty marks he feels happy and says to himself: "Good, my face is clean."
>
> In the same way, my friends, if we look deeply and see unwholesome states that have not yet been transformed,

we should practice diligently in order to transform them. If we look deeply and see that all unwholesome states have already been transformed, we can feel joyful about this and continue to practice diligently in order to nourish and cultivate this wholesome state.

The Sangha is our mirror, our fellow practitioners are our mirror, and our family members are our mirror. Practicing with humility and openness we can make great progress by making use of the mirrors that others show to us. In confronting our weaknesses and finding ways to overcome them, we will feel light. When we observe a particular behavior in ourselves, we can ask others for support: "Dear elder brother, dear younger sister, please help me. When you see that I am behaving in such and such a way please give me a sign." When we ask for support like this, our family members or our Sangha members will have great respect and love for us and they will be encouraged to do the same.

Accepting the Dharma Medicine

Some people do not know how to accept medicine when they have a physical or mental illness. When the medication is given, they find ways to run away. Likewise, some people are afraid of listening to a Dharma talk or reading a sutra because they fear that it may touch painful areas in them. The Dharma has the nature of dealing directly with reality. When a Dharma talk touches such painful matters, we feel our happiness is lost. We might wish to run away or to listen to teachings only on abstract theories.

But sometimes while reading a sutra or listening to a Dharma talk, we will find the kind of healing that we deeply need. If, when we hear the teachings that can help us the most, we only think in circles, we may prevent the Dharma rain from penetrating and healing us. We may think the teaching would be good for our brother or our wife to hear, but that we ourselves do not need it. Or we may think that since the teaching was given a long time ago, it is not relevant for our current situation.

The teaching words of the Buddha are called "the all-embracing sound." This means that the words have the nature of fullness, touching all kinds of human conditions. All-embracing sound also means that the words of the Buddha have the characteristic of being appropriate to the hearer. Because it is an all-embracing sound, it can touch our real situation. To receive the all-embracing sound we need to cultivate our capacity to listen with openness, receptivity, and stillness. Listening in this way, we will surely receive the medicine we need.

Creating Harmony and Happiness

T HE VINAYA, the collection of precepts, is the basis for the guidelines of the sangha and provides the foundation for the harmony and happiness of the sangha body.

The Development of the Three Collections of Buddhist Scripture

Buddha's teachings were not written down during his lifetime. Instead, his disciples learned them all by heart and transmitted them orally from one generation to the next. This began three months after the Buddha entered nirvana and in the eighth year of the rule of Ajatasattu, when the Venerable Kassapa[1] decided to call together a council of the five hundred senior disciples of the Buddha who were outstanding in their practice and their studies. They were chosen from the different bhikshu Sanghas and came to the capital city of Rajagriha to recite and collate all the teachings of the Buddha. King Ajatasattu agreed to sponsor this collation. The great gathering opened at the beginning of the rains retreat that year and lasted for six months.

In the great gathering, the assembly invited the Venerable Upali, who was well known for his study of the mindfulness trainings,[2] to recite the whole of the monastic discipline, known as the *Vinaya Pitaka,* as it existed at that time.[3]

Thanks to questions from Venerable Kassapa and the Sangha, the Venerable Upali was able to remember all the causes and conditions that led the Buddha to establish each mindfulness training.

Then, the assembly invited Venerable Ananda to recite all the Dharma talks, or sutras, that the Buddha had spoken. Thanks to the questions and support of the Venerable Kassapa and the 500 bhikshus who had reached understanding and attainment in the Dharma, Ananda was also able to recite all the details concerning the time, the place, and the situation for which the Buddha delivered each discourse.

At this first council, the whole of the teachings of the Buddha were recited and gathered into the "three baskets" of teachings called the sutras, the Vinaya, and the shastra.[4] This was possible thanks to the Venerables Upali, Ananda, and the 500 bhikshus who were outstanding in their study and practice.

One hundred years later, seven hundred arhats met a second time. There was a third council 236 years later in order to recite and supplement the teachings of the Buddha. According to the Theravada, or Southern, school of Buddhism, in the year 83 B.C.E. under the reign of King Vatta Gamini Abhaya of Sri Lanka, a group of arhats gathered one more time in Aluvihara, a small town about thirty kilometers from Kandi on the island of Sri Lanka.[5]

This was a fourth gathering of the leaders of the Buddha's Sangha and the first time that the three *pitaka*s were written down on palm leaves in the Pali language. When published in book form today, they are about eleven times thicker than the Christian Bible.

The Monastic Constitution

The Buddha said to his disciples: "After I have passed into nirvana, the precepts and the discipline will take my place as your teacher. Wherever there is the monastic discipline with its mindfulness trainings, I am there. If the Sangha practices the mindfulness trainings correctly, then my teachings will stay with you life after life. If not, the teachings I have given you will only remain in the world for a very short time." That is why it is important for practitioners who wish to build the Sangha to study and understand the monastic discipline.

The vinaya forms the basis for the regulations of a Sangha, allowing it to be a place of refuge. These precepts, in accordance with the spirit of the Dharma, also provide the foundation for the harmony and happiness of the Sangha body.

For many years after he had realized awakening, the Buddha did not establish fixed mindfulness trainings for his Sangha. Instead, he gave suitable warnings to the monks and nuns whenever they were needed. Then, after some time, he began to make precepts, or mindfulness trainings, as clear guidelines for monastic life that could be followed by all monks and nuns in the community. This is how the monastic discipline evolved. The text of the discipline contains descriptions of all the reasons and the different circumstances for which the Buddha established each mindfulness training. We should know the origin of each mindfulness training and the conditions under which it was set up so that when we practice the training we will not go in the wrong direction and apply it incorrectly. In the vinaya we also find descriptions of the different types of confession and repentance, or Beginning Anew, in the Sangha.

Two of the terms we use are "mindfulness trainings" and "monastic discipline." Sometimes we talk about them as one thing, "trainings and discipline." Nevertheless, trainings are a little bit different from discipline. Mindfulness trainings are called "sila" in Sanskrit. Sila means actions, practices, and ethics in our daily lives. In English we can also translate sila as "precepts" or "morality," and recently we have been translating it as "mindfulness trainings." These guidelines exist to help us stay on the right path, keeping us safe and protecting our freedom.

In Sanskrit monastic discipline is called "vinaya." This includes the many specific regulations, statutes, and rules that help the monastic community to live together in harmony and happiness. They help us put into practice the Buddha's teachings and to overcome our difficulties and our confusion. The monastic discipline is very broad. It includes the mindfulness trainings, but it covers a much wider field. The vinaya could be called the constitution of the Sangha.

We have to study it regularly in order to be able to master it fully. In the monastic community, those who have fully mastered the monastic discipline are called "vinaya masters." If the Sangha's practice is to be of high quality, there should be vinaya masters as part of the community. In Vietnam, both historically and today, there are always a number of monks and nuns who are well-versed in the vinaya. To fully master the study of the discipline, you must spend at least five years solely studying the vinaya.

According to the Buddhist texts, there have to be at least four bhikshus or bhikshunis to recite the monastic discipline for monks or nuns, the *Pratimoksha*. These four people must have received *upasampada,* or full ordination. Monks receive the 250 mindfulness trainings of the bhikshu, and nuns receive the 348 mindfulness trainings of the bhikshuni. A Sangha like this is the smallest "official" Sangha. Naturally, when there are not four bhikshus or bhikshunis in the Sangha, we can still continue to study and practice, but, according to the monastic discipline, we do not have the right to perform certain functions. An even larger Sangha is required to perform functions like the full ordination ceremony or the *pavarana* ceremony at the end of every rains retreat.[6]

A Sangha of at least twenty bhikshus or bhikshunis is permitted to perform all the functions prescribed in the *Vinaya Pitaka.*

Updating the Monastic Code

On March 31, 2003, at the Sangha University in Seoul, Korea, the Plum Village monastics released a revised version of the *Pratimoksha.* This is a revolutionary step, as it is the first time in 2,600 years that the vinaya has been updated to meet the situations and needs of our present-day monastic communities.

I firmly believe that the Buddha needs courageous disciples to continue his teachings and to make the Buddhist tradition alive and vital for young people today. Buddhism is a living reality. Like a tree, the dead branches need to be pruned in order to allow new shoots to grow. The new shoots are the teachings that are appropriate to our time and culture. Developments in technology have penetrated the monastic world. Corruption in different monastic orders, both Buddhist and non-Buddhist, is evident in many places. A revised *Pratimoksha* was urgently needed to deal with these situations. Cars, computers, television, electronic games, and the Internet are all addressed within the 250 precepts of the revised *Pratimoksha*. The release of the revised *Pratimoksha* is a cultural event that should be of interest to many spiritual traditions.

In the revised *Pratimoksha,* there is a mindfulness training stating that, within one year of receiving the full ordination, we should study the traditional *Pratimoksha* along with the revised version. Studying the traditional *Pratimoksha* connects us to the original Sangha of the Buddha, as the precepts and the situations leading to their creation were in the time of the Buddha. We feel very humble when we see all the mistakes that monks and nuns made at that time. Because of their mistakes and shortcomings, the Buddha had the opportunity to offer many mindfulness trainings to help us avoid difficulties on the path of practice.

The revised version was also created in response to real situations, mistakes, and shortcomings of monastics in our contemporary period. Many of the traditional trainings have been kept, though their language has been updated and made clearer. A number of mindfulness trainings have been added to address circumstances that did not exist in the time of the Buddha. Likewise, trainings that are no longer applicable to our current situation have been dropped. But we do not need to feel that we have lost anything, as the traditional *Pratimoksha* is still available for us to consult and study.

I would recommend that every twenty years an assembly of monastics gathers to look deeply into the *Pratimoksha* and the current needs of the monastic community to revise the precepts to keep them alive and fresh. When the mindfulness trainings are stated in such a way that we can easily understand and apply them, we receive more energy for our practice.

Decision-Making for the Happiness and Harmony of the Community

The way we make decisions on all matters that arise in the Sangha is called *"sanghakarman"* procedure. This is a very good practice for reaching consensus with our brothers and sisters. The person who is guiding a community of practice should master the details of this procedure. The sanghakarman procedure helps the Sangha organize its life of spiritual practice successfully and make decisions harmoniously. *Karma* means "action" or "activity." The Chinese words for this procedure are *zuo fa ban shi,* which mean "taking action." In English we might say "making a decision." Action here is collective and not individual, because the decision is a collective decision taken by the whole community. All decisions in a Buddhist community of practice have to be based on the sanghakarman procedure. These procedures are found in the vinaya.

The success of a majority of Sangha activities depends on the use of the sanghakarman procedure. Whenever there are urgent matters to be decided in the Sangha, even if it's not possible to gather the whole Sangha for a meeting, we should call an emergency meeting of bhikshus or bhikshunis who happen to be present at the time in order to realize the sanghakarman procedure. However urgent a matter is, we do not leave any important decision for one person to decide, even if that person is the abbot or the head of the community.

There are three methods of karman procedure. The first is called the "mental karman procedure." This procedure is carried out in our mind if we are alone. For example, when we find ourselves in a situation where we have to practice alone, we can use the karman procedure. In this case, we see that the rules can be quite wide and embracing of many circumstances. For example, usually we do a karman procedure to announce the beginning of a rains retreat, or to announce that we will recite the mindfulness trainings. With the mental karman procedure we can still perform these functions when we are alone. We prostrate to the Buddha and Sangha in our hearts, and then we mentally recite the karman by ourselves.

The second kind of karman procedure is called "face-to-face karman." We use face-to-face karman when we have with us only one or two other people. Although this too is not considered complete according to the monastic discipline of the Buddha, it is still suitable when we are fewer than four gathered together.

The third karman procedure is called "sanghakarman." It is the karman procedure most in accord with the teachings of the Buddha because there are at least three other bhikshus or bhikshunis with us.

The sanghakarman procedure itself also has three different forms. The first is called the "single announcement karman," or *natti kamma* in Pali. In the daily activities of the Sangha, there are many simple matters to be decided. For these, the sanghakarman master, or another person who has responsibility for the matter at hand, invites a sound of the bell, stands up before the community, and makes a simple announcement of the decision. If no one raises any objection, the decision is automatically put into effect by the whole Sangha.

For example, after the Sangha has had their midday meal, a sister might stand up, invite the sound of the bell, and state: "Respected Sangha, today we will not have a tea meditation as usual because we have to prepare for the grand ordination ceremony." In this case, one or two people might ask: "Why can we not have both the tea ceremony and the preparation?" The sister who has made the announcement will explain why, and because the matter is not very important, the community will feel no need for a meeting to arrive at a consensus. There are some traditional monasteries where just by using this "single announcement" procedure, the bhikshus and bhikshunis are able to resolve half of all decisions concerning the daily activities of the Sangha.

An important part of this procedure is that someone always announces these decisions to the Sangha. If our brothers and sisters don't know what has been decided, they may reproach us, asking why we went ahead and did something without announcing it first. This is a principle we must obey to preserve the atmosphere of harmony, peace, and happiness in the Sangha.

The second type of sanghakarman procedure is called "double announcement karman," or *natti dutiya kamma* in Pali. This means that an announcement has to be made twice, and it is used for more important decisions that need clear agreement from the whole Sangha. For example, a brother may address the Sangha after the meal, saying, "Respected Sangha, because of pressing need, a number of those responsible for the organization of the community have proposed that we recite the mindfulness trainings next Tuesday instead of this Friday as usual. This change will be effective only for one week. I present this proposal to you."

In this sanghakarman procedure, we first clearly present the proposition and the reason for it. Then we state: "This is the wording of the announcement. Is it clear?" That is called the first announcement. If it is clear, the Sangha will reply: "Clear." Then the announcement will be repeated just as it was made the first time. After it has been repeated, we ask: "Respected Sangha, are you happy to accept this proposition?" This is the second announcement. If anyone has a concern about the issue, they must speak up. In this case, we may postpone the decision for further discussion. If everyone is silent, we will say: "The Sangha is silent. Therefore we know that the Sangha has accepted the proposition, and we understand that we can go ahead and put it into effect."

For example, reciting the mindfulness trainings is an important practice. If someone fails to be present at the recitation and does not send their wish to be represented by another, that brother or sister has transgressed the precepts. That is why we must use the sanghakarman procedure with a double announcement for this important decision. In the vinaya of the Dharmagupta school[7], there are about seventy-eight cases in which the Sangha has to use the double announcement procedure.

The third type of sanghakarman procedure is called "quadruple announcement," or *natti catuttha kamma* in Pali. It includes an announcement followed by three repetitions of the question to be decided. There are forty cases in the vinaya where this sanghakarman procedure must be used. It is reserved for very important decisions when the Sangha needs time to think carefully, such as the decision to allow someone to receive ordination (novice or full ordination) or become a long-term resident of the community. These are important matters because whether that person is able to receive the precepts or stay as a long-term resident relates greatly to the happiness of the whole Sangha.

Is There Harmony in the Sangha?

Here is an example of the quadruple announcement sanghakarman procedure performed for the ordination of novice monks and nuns:

> Sanghakarman master: Has the entire community assembled?
> Convocation master: Yes, the entire community has assembled.
> Sanghakarman master: Is there harmony in the community?
> Convocation master: Yes, there is harmony.
> Sanghakarman master: Why has the community assembled today?
> Convocation master: The community has assembled today in order to give spiritual support to the ordination ceremony and to realize the sanghakarman of transmitting the novice precepts.
> Sanghakarman master: Venerable bhikshus and bhikshunis, please listen. The ordinees with the following Dharma names are requesting to receive the novice precepts, and they have invited the Venerable (first name) (second name) to be their Upadhyaya[8]. The ordinees whose names have been read have shown that they are practicing the

mindfulness trainings and that there is no impediment to their being ordained. If you see that this is the right time for the ordination and there is no obstacle to its taking place, then please, Venerables, allow these ordinees to receive the novice precepts. This is the announcement. Is this announcement clear?

The whole community: Clear.

Sanghakarman master: Venerable bhikshus and bhikshunis, please listen. The ordinees with the following Dharma names are requesting to receive . . . (repeated as above). Please allow these ordinees to receive the novice precepts. Whoever in the Sangha accepts this proposal please be silent, and whoever does not accept the proposal, please speak out (pause). This is the first time of asking.

Sanghakarman master: (Repeat as above.) This is the second time of asking.

Sanghakarman master: (Repeat as above.) This is the third time of asking.

Sanghakarman master: Noble Sangha, the bhikshus and bhikshunis have been silent after being asked three times. We know therefore that everyone accepts the proposal. The sanghakarman procedure for the ordination of the novices has therefore been realized.

Every time we perform a sanghakarman procedure we ask, is there harmony in the community? This should not be an empty question. Harmony is the essence of a Sangha, of a community of practice. Harmony is not something that we achieve perfectly, but it, like the mindfulness trainings, is a guiding light that we are always practicing and moving toward. All the activities of the Sangha are for the purpose of cultivating harmony. When we sit together in silent meditation, cook together, clean together, and make decisions together we are building our harmony and our capacity to understand, accept, and love each other as brothers and sisters.

Being in harmony does not mean that we do not disagree or make mistakes and miss opportunities to understand one another. It means that we are doing our best and there is no division or split within the Sangha. We are sincerely practicing the way of liberation and peace for ourselves and for each other. We never forget our commitment to each other, our commitment to ourselves to practice mindfulness night and day, dwelling happily in the present moment. That is the teaching of the *Sutra on Knowing the Better Way to Live Alone.*[9] Harmony is our daily practice; it is our most essential practice.

Arriving at Agreement in the Sangha

There are cases when the sanghakarman procedure cannot be realized because someone opposes the proposal. In this case the matter at hand cannot go forward. Any bhikshu or bhikshuni who practices the mindfulness trainings correctly may present their opposition to the motion in the spirit of the mindfulness trainings. This is their right to veto. When this happens, we adjourn the proceedings. If we cannot find harmony on this question, we do not hurry to reassemble the Sangha. We take our time to listen to the views of everyone concerned until a consensus is reached, at which point we can reinitiate the sanghakarman procedure.

In general, it is best to ask for the input and advice of a number of people in the community, to find out if there is a split in the Sangha before performing a sanghakarman procedure. This means that we have already included the ideas and insight of members of the community to form the proposal we will offer to the community. We can have formal meetings in which everyone assembles and each member offers his or her view on a particular issue. For example, when the community is considering whether or not to ordain an aspiring nun or not, all the nuns in that community will sit together. Each nun will offer her insights about the aspirant and state whether she supports her ordination or not. Once every community member shares her view, if one or more sisters disagree, others in the community might try to persuade them to follow the majority. Perhaps listening to their sisters' views, they will change their minds. Otherwise, they may say that they will follow the Sangha. This means that although they have some reservations, they will accept the strength of the majority's opinion and will not oppose the decision. Once there is unanimous approval, it is clear that the aspirant can be accepted for ordination.

At other times, the Sangha may need to postpone a decision to allow the situation to evolve and to gather more information. Only after there is a clear consensus among the community will a decision be carried out. So at the moment of ordination when the sanghakarman procedure is performed, the monks and nuns have already gone through a process of sharing and harmonizing their views and they are aware of the proposal that will be made. The sanghakarman procedure is thus a formalized declaration of a decision that has already been thought about for sometime and for which a consensus has already been reached within the community. We can say that the sanghakarman procedure legalizes the decision of the Sangha. Because of this it is rare that anyone objects to the realization of a sanghakarman procedure.

When a sanghakarman procedure is realized, everyone bows and says out loud, "realized." Thus, with a verbal and physical gesture, everyone offers his or her assent and support to the action that is being taken. This is a powerful statement of inclusiveness and participation in the Sangha life.

The Right to Vote and the Right to Veto

Traditionally, the head of the community has the right to veto. He or she will be a master of the monastic discipline and understand the teachings very deeply. When the head of the community sees that the Sangha is making a decision that is not in accord with the teachings, he can block the decision. In the past, when I have seen that the decision of the Sangha is not in accord with the spirit of the tradition, I have sometimes said: "Venerable bhikshus and bhikhsunis, although you have reached consensus on this matter, there are certain aspects which have not been seen clearly. Let us postpone making any decision today. Once I have had an opportunity to help the Sangha see more clearly, you will be in a much better position to come to the right decision."

The head of a community should use the right to veto only in very serious matters. If we operated on our bodies every time they were a little sick, we would be in a great deal of pain and would not have very much strength. The best thing for an abbot or an abbess to do is to ask the Sangha to adjourn for a day so that he or she has a chance to share his or her point of view and the long experience of the Buddhist monastic tradition. When she has more time to present her insight, her sisters may see that their decision was not appropriate.

There are also some limits to the right to veto. A novice does not have the right to veto a matter being decided by bhikshus or bhikshunis unless that novice has already been accepted as an ordinee for the next full ordination ceremony. Similarly, any bhikshu or bhikshuni who is away from the monastery when a meeting is happening —even a member of the Sangha who is practicing the mindfulness trainings purely—does not have the right to vote or to veto. Nor does he or she have the right to use the telephone, postal correspondence, e-mail, or other means of communication to express opposition to any proposal in a meeting. For example, even a bhikshuni whose train is late returning to the monastery in time for a meeting, no matter how important her opinion might be, does not have the right to veto. This is laid down in the text on monastic discipline of the Buddha.

Similarly, when we have sanghakarman proceedings, all members of the Sangha in the meeting must sit near enough to be able to reach out and touch the other members. If someone is sitting even five or seven meters away, that person does not have the right to vote or to veto. This is the custom as laid down in the monastic discipline of the

Buddha. Perhaps this is so that everyone is near enough to hear each other clearly and to contribute their physical support and presence to the Sangha meeting. When we sit far away from the Sangha—in a Dharma talk, in a meeting or during meal time—we are making a statement about being distanced from the Sangha. Sometimes we need to take some space within the Sangha body. That is not wrong. But in the context of an important Sangha meeting we should offer our full presence and attention so that the harmony and togetherness is maintained and the decision can be made without difficulty.

Reaching a Harmony of Views in the Sangha

The same spirit of consensus that was alive in the Sangha some 2,600 years ago continues today. This is why, when we organize a sanghakarman procedure in order to determine a very important matter in the Sangha, those who have responsibility for the meeting should first understand the different opinions among their brothers and sisters and gather them together at the appropriate time. Everyone in the Sangha must have the opportunity to offer their views and to present their ideas.

Calling for a meeting of the Sangha in order to listen to everyone explain their ideas is a basic and necessary practice. Those who have been ordained a long time have the duty to encourage their younger brothers and sisters to express their opinions. Only when the younger members of the Sangha are able to contribute their ideas naturally and with ease can good decisions be made. When the younger members of the community learn how to contribute their insights to the running of the Sangha, the Sangha has a future. The idea that "children should be seen and not heard" is destructive both in the life of the family and the life of the Sangha. Please listen with the ears of the Buddha to all members of the Sangha. When we practice in this way, a meeting will be successful in bringing about peace and happiness in the community.

During a meeting, someone, even the abbot, may think that the

Sangha has made a decision that is not completely sound. Even so, it is important for us all to agree to follow the decisions of the Sangha. The Sangha has the Sangha eyes and the Sangha ears and generally makes the best decision. After a while, we may even see that the Sangha was right and we were wrong. We have taken refuge in the Sangha, and so we must place our trust in it. In the monastery or in our families, taking refuge in the community is not just a proclamation or an aspiration. It is our daily practice. If everyone practices according to this principle, peace and joy will be possible.

This does not mean you should not share your opinion. You will feel at a loss if you have not been able to share everything that is in your heart during a meeting. But after you have presented everything in your heart, you agree to follow the Sangha even if the decision does not correspond with your opinion. You know that your contribution has been heard and you have trust in the wisdom of the collective insight that will arise from everyone's input. You also trust in the senior members of the community to take in all the different viewpoints and find a harmonious outcome that will benefit the entire community.

When you can lay aside your personal idea for the sake of harmony in the Sangha, this is the practice of the harmony of ideas. For example, when the majority has come to a consensus and you are not wholly in agreement, you can go along with the consensus so that the harmony of the Sangha is not affected. This often happens at Plum Village. Even as the senior teacher in the community, sometimes I do not agree entirely with an idea of the Sangha, but I tell myself: "This decision is good enough. Allowing the Sangha to make this decision will help the Sangha to grow."

Another important practice is called "togetherness of views to bring joy." Whenever we can, as many of us as possible should sit together in order for our insight about each other to grow. This will enable us to come to the right decision for our community more easily. If we need more time to find a decision that will make everyone happy, then we should be patient enough to sit together in another meeting to hear more ideas.

Whatever the outcome of a decision, if there is still something that you feel you need to share with the Sangha, you should find the time to do this later. You can look for an opportunity to share your insight so that next time the decision will be better. If you share your opinion with loving speech and the right motivation, you will remove the possibility of dispute and opposition, which can harm the life of the Sangha.

CHAPTER 4

The Seven Methods of Resolving Conflicts

The Seven Ways to Remove Disputes and Conflicts

THE LAST SEVEN of the 250 precepts for a monk can be called the "Seven Ways to Remove Disputes and Conflicts" in the Sangha. If we know how to use these teachings and practices, we can help restore harmony, happiness, and joy in the Sangha, in the family, and even in the community of all nations.

The First Practice of Removing Conflicts
All parties should be present in a meeting to share their suffering.

The first practice is to have all parties present in a meeting so that everyone has a chance to tell what is on his or her mind—the suffering he or she has undergone. The whole Sangha then practices deep listening. During this deep listening there is no discussing. This is very different from a peace conference at which one person says something and the other side answers. The full presence of all parties is very important. The whole community should also be present so that everyone has a chance to say what is in his heart, especially his suffering.

This can be practiced in many types of communities. If the Security Council of the United Nations thinks that they need the presence of the leaders of two warring nations, for example, then they would issue an invitation for both leaders to come to a meeting with their assistants. The community of all nations would just sit together and listen. They could listen to each leader—his suffering, his worries, his fears, his intentions, why he has done what he has done in the past, why he is contemplating what he is going to do now, and so on. Every ambassador would have to sit and listen without any prejudices, since the purpose is not to establish who is right and who is wrong; the purpose is to listen deeply.

In a Sangha where people practice mindfulness, this practice of deep listening to both sides may not be so difficult. We know how to listen with compassion, to hear the truth without opposing one side and supporting the other. Do you think that ambassadors to the UN are capable of listening like that? If they have not been trained, they will support their own side and oppose the other side. That is not peace, but its opposite.

If we are truly motivated to create peace in the world, if we deeply want a peaceful solution, then we should abandon our habit of supporting one side over the other. Please practice deep listening with equanimity and without prejudice. We have the tendency to think that only we suffer, but when we sit and listen deeply to the other side we may find out that they too suffer.

In the family, if two members in the family are in conflict, we can organize this kind of meeting. If there is a conflict in our community, then we have to convene a meeting with the presence of both parties and we just practice deep listening. Without coming to any decision, that session of deep listening can already release a lot of tension and misunderstanding in the minds of everyone concerning the nature of the conflict. Practicing deep listening will dissipate a lot of wrong understanding and wrong perceptions. This is already the path of peace.

We can translate the original text of the precept like this: *If there is a need to convene the entire Sangha with the presence of both parties in order to settle the dispute, then we convene the Sangha in order to listen to the two concerned parties.* Maybe in the future, every ambassador who will be sent to the UN will go to an international institute of training in deep listening and loving speech. After having that certificate he will be qualified to be nominated as an ambassador. It is up to us to decide. You don't have to be a Buddhist to see the value of this practice.

At one time, in many Asian countries, such as Thailand, you could not get married unless you had spent one year in the temple, to add a spiritual dimension in your life. The prince also, before he was allowed to be a king, had to undergo one year of practice in the temple. That is a very good thing. Here we don't need a temple, but we need a kind of institute where politicians can spend time in order to learn how to recognize the seeds of compassion, the seeds of anger, and try to learn basic things like mindful breathing, mindful embracing of our anger and so on. That is what we can call civilization. If you are a good writer, please write an article telling people that you don't need to be a Buddhist in order to support this. An international institute for diplomats and statesmen is possible. The European parliament could bring this into the agenda and discuss the topic of such an institute.

The Second Practice of Removing Conflicts
All parties should remember and recount the details of the conflict.

The second practice is remembrance. Listening has the capacity of helping the concerned parties to suffer less, and to feel they are being understood by others. It's possible a meeting needs to be convened in order to encourage the concerned people to remember everything that has happened in the past. In this way, whatever they have seen, heard, and thought about can be expressed to the community. Before speaking in public, a person needs to sit down quietly and to remember. Members of the Sangha can ask him or her to remember and to provide as many details as possible of the base of the conflict. This is a way to help everyone, including the concerned parties, to look deeply.

In the first practice, you need only to tell what is in your mind, your suffering. The second practice is to urge the person to remember and to see how the suffering has come about. This is an opportunity to see that the suffering has not come only from the behavior of the other person but it has come also from our own unskillfulness and our own way of thinking. The Sangha will have a chance to shed light for the person to better understand himself and the other party.

The text of the second practice reads as follows: *If we need to convene a meeting in order to urge the other person to remember and to tell us what he has thought, what he has heard, what he has done, what he has seen concerning the conflict, then we will convene that meeting.*

The first practice can help bring about the fruit of reconciliation. If the first practice has helped but has not brought the result that we want, then we can use the second practice so that everyone can see his or her responsibility in the conflict, rather than just blaming the other person for his or her own suffering.

The Third Practice of Removing Conflicts
It should be determined that neither party is mentally ill.

The third practice is determining sanity. You must be sure that the concerned party is not mentally ill. When you are not well mentally you might do and say things that create suffering for other people and for yourself. If a person says that he doesn't remember anything because he was in a state of deep disturbance, then the Sangha will settle the dispute. The Sangha may say something like: "You should not condemn this person because he was in a state of mind where he could not control himself."

The Fourth Practice of Removing Conflicts
The parties should confess their own unskillfulness.

The fourth practice is self confession. If there is a need to convene a meeting so that the concerned party can speak about the unskillfulness and the lack of mindfulness that has led him or her to do or say what has done damage in the Sangha, then we have to organize a meeting for the concerned person to do so. This is very good. In any conflict there is a tendency to escalate the conflict. You condemn the other person and he or she condemns you and you escalate the level of anger. But this practice is different. The concerned person might say something like this: "Dear Sangha, dear friends, it was my fault. I was not very mindful, I was not very compassionate, I was not skillful and that is why I have done such a thing that has caused misunderstanding. I have said such a thing that has offended my brother or my sister. I am truly sorry. I would like to express my regret."

This is what we do in our practice of Beginning Anew.[1] We invite the other party to do the same. The other person, our adversary, may see that we are capable of de-escalating. We are able to recognize some of our own weaknesses and unskillfulness and he will be encouraged to do the same. This will de-escalate our anger and the conflict. This practice is especially beneficial when we are brothers and sisters who live closely together. When we are unskillful and we allow our feelings to dominate us, we can use the practice of admitting our own unskillfulness to allow the feeling of brotherhood and sisterhood, the true love between us, to express itself again. This is the practice of de-escalation. The de-escalation of one party will bring about the de-escalation of the other party.

No one among us is perfect. Our leaders are not perfect. No nation is perfect. We have done wrong to ourselves, we have done wrong to our fellow nations. If we want to practice deep listening this is not difficult at all. America can say: "We are not perfect. We have made many mistakes in our foreign policy. If we have made you suffer we apologize. Please tell us more about our unskillfulness." If America could say something like that, then any other country could also say something like that. That is de-escalation. It can be done in the context of the community of all nations, the United Nations. If we consider ourselves to be civilized people, why aren't we capable of acting like that? In our practice of Beginning Anew we always come forth and express our regret first and this calms everyone's feelings.

The Fifth Practice of Removing Conflicts
A committee is assembled to investigate the nature of the conflict.

The fifth method of resolving conflict is to inquire more about the nature of the conflict and of the wrongdoing. If there is a need to confide the matter to a jury, a group of people, in order to study and understand the case in all its details, then we have to do this. If the Sangha does not have the time to go into the many details of the conflict, especially if the conflict has been there for a long time, then the Sangha will assign a group of people in order to make a deep study of the case. After some time, whether it is three weeks or two months, that jury will give a full report and the Sangha will make a decision according to their report.

In the case of the situation in the Middle East, the United Nations could assign a group of people to study the conflicts in depth. The group could be composed of experts on international affairs, including jurists, politicians, and spiritual leaders because we also need a spiritual dimension in the process. That jury should be agreed upon by the Sangha, especially by the people in conflict. We should allow that jury to do their job. The United Nations can base their decisions on the jury's insight and this will help solve the conflicts.

The Sixth Practice of Removing Conflicts
A majority vote is used to resolve the conflict.

The sixth method is to use a majority vote to solve the problem. If the report given by the jury does not satisfy everyone, then the United Nations will have to solve the problem with a majority vote. The same thing is true in the Sangha. Suppose the brothers who were assigned to study the case have done so, and afterwards they report the case. If the other brothers say, "We don't feel that the whole truth has been brought out, but we know the jury has done their best," then the brothers have to come together and settle the dispute by voting. After the settlement, the matter is considered closed. Once a verdict has been pronounced, you no longer have any right to bring up the old affair and make it into an issue. According to the Buddhist monastic code, that is an offense.

In the Buddhist context, it is better if there is a unanimous vote. If you really practice taking refuge in the Sangha, then you have to surrender your view. If your brothers are in the great majority and if you don't give up your views, you could be splitting the community. Splitting the Sangha is a great offense. If you ask a number of people to follow you to oppose the vote and if you maintain that situation of the minority opposing the majority, you are committing the offense of splitting the Sangha. The Buddha created that precept in order to encourage everyone to make every effort to maintain harmony in the community. We know that harmony in the community is the solid foundation for our happiness and for the transformation and healing of all the members of the community.

The Seventh Practice of Removing Conflicts
Respected senior members of the community are invited to declare a general amnesty.

The seventh practice is general amnesty. This means laying down the straw to cover the muddy ground. It is not pleasant to walk on a muddy path. When there is a lot of mud on the path you will spoil your shoes. That was the situation at Plum Village fifteen years ago. Now we have done our best to make paths that you can walk on. At that time, however, we didn't have enough straw so we used wooden planks. We used everything we could find to put over the mud so that we could walk across it. The seventh method of resolving conflicts is the same.

You convene a meeting. You invite the most respected elders in your community to be present, even if he or she is very old. The elder wise ones come because they see that you cannot resolve the conflict. You just listen to the wise ones and they will say something like this: "We are all brothers and sisters of the same family. We have to forgive each other. We have to put down straw on the muddy path so that we can walk together. I propose a general amnesty."

Everyone involved in the conflict prostrates before the wise ones and forgets the conflict. This is the most wonderful practice among the seven. I don't know whether they can do such a practice in the United Nations. They should have a highly respected elder who is full of compassion. When you hear such a person speak you just bow down and you follow what is recommended, whichever party you support. The seed of compassion in you is touched and you accept the other person and you accept the amnesty. You don't have the need to see the other person punished anymore.

This is the way of the Buddha. The monastics have recited these seven ways of resolving conflicts for 2,600 years. This is a wonderful teaching and practice that is still applicable and effective in the present moment. If you are a jurist, a lawyer, or a writer, please write an article on these seven ways of resolving disputes, because the light of the Buddha can still be used in order to solve the problems of our times.

❧ CHAPTER 5
Caring for Each Other

P LUM VILLAGE is a meditation center established in 1982. It is one
hour's drive from the town of Bordeaux in southwest France. In
its first years the meditation center was called Persimmon Village
because of all its persimmon trees. Later on, young Vietnamese practitioners from all over the world came to learn about the practice,
and they offered their pocket money to buy and plant 1,250 plum
trees to represent the 1,250 monastics in the original Sangha of the
Buddha. From then on the center has been called Plum Village, or *le
Village des Pruniers* in French.

The "root temple" of Plum Village is Tu Hieu Temple in Vietnam,
where our meditation lineage began.[1] We at Plum Village are descen-
dants of the Tu Hieu Temple. I still remember the day when I was a
young novice aspirant, sitting and weeding the garden around the
half-moon lake in front of the temple. Even today, in my mind I can
see clearly the image of the early morning mist floating over the lotus
lake through the temple's three portals. Now, at Plum Village, I am
an elder in our lineage, and after thirty years of practicing Sangha
building, the Sangha body of Plum Village includes monks and nuns
of many different nationalities in many countries.

Plum Village is like a new branch on the large, ancient tree of the
Tu Hieu lineage. The Dharma doors of Plum Village have made its
teachings, descended from the Lin Chi school in China,[2] clearer and
more accessible to people of this present time. Plum Village has established a tradition of meditation practice that is widely accepted among
both Buddhists and those who do not call themselves Buddhists. Tens

of thousands of people from Europe, America, Russia, Australia, China, Japan, Korea, Israel, and other countries around the world have asked to receive and are putting into practice the Five Mindfulness Trainings. There are more than 800 local Sanghas that practice in the Plum Village tradition and more than 200 permanent residents studying and practicing in the main practice centers of the Tu Hieu lineage overseas. Many members of these local Sanghas also belong to the Tiep Hien Order (the Order of Interbeing) and have received the fourteen precepts of the order. All these brothers and sisters belong to the forty-third generation of the Lin Chi school and to the ninth generation of the Lieu Quang[3] Dharma line.

Plum Village consists of four year-round hamlets: the Upper Hamlet (or Dharma Cloud Temple) for monks and laymen is in Thenac; the New Hamlet (or Loving Kindness Temple), where the nuns live, is in the village of Dieulivol; the Lower Hamlet (or Dharma Nectar Temple), also for nuns, is found near the village of Loubes-Bernac. Laywomen also live in both of these hamlets. Most recently, Foot of the Mountain Temple for monks was founded adjacent to the Upper Hamlet. Apart from the four main hamlets, the West Hamlet, the Middle Hamlet, and the New Hamlet's Gate House and Hillside House are open only during large retreats.

The Plum Village Sangha also includes two centers in the United States. The Vermont center includes Maple Forest Monastery, founded in September 1997, and Green Mountain Dharma Center, founded in April 1998. Green Mountain Dharma Center is reserved for nuns and laywomen, and Maple Forest Monastery, also called Stone Boy Hamlet, is reserved for monks and laymen. The second center in the U.S. is called Deer Park Monastery, founded in July 2000. It is in southern California near Escondido, which means "hidden among the mountains," so it is called the Monastery Hidden among the Mountains. It has two hamlets: Solidity Hamlet for the monks and Clarity Hamlet for the nuns.

There is also a small hamlet in Berlin, Germany, which monastics come to for part of the year to offer support to the local Sanghas. The monastics do not spend Winter Retreat there, though, so it is not a full time monastery. It is called Source of Compassion or *Suoi Thuong* in Vietnamese.

The Plum Village Sangha Structure

When practicing to build the Sangha in Plum Village, we combine the spirit of seniority with the spirit of democracy. The tradition of seniority in Buddhism teaches that those who have been ordained longer have more experience in the monastic life. Their understanding is usually greater, and they are more capable of making better decisions. In every monastery, elders, called Mahathera or Thera, are trusted because of their experience and wisdom. When we rely on them to make decisions for the community, we are applying the principle of seniority. According to the democratic spirit, we also trust that everyone, both experienced and inexperienced, has a contribution to make to the decisions of the Sangha.

At Plum Village, we combine the principles of seniority and democracy so that everyone in the community has the right to offer their experience and ideas. In the old tradition, the elders, especially the abbot, usually decided everything. In today's democracies, everyone should be encouraged to express their points of view. In our community there is an abbot or abbess, a caretaking council, and a Dharmacharya council. There is also the assembly of bhikshus and bhikshunis. It is like a constitutional monarchy, with a monarch, a parliament, and a government. The government executes the laws that come from the decisions made by the parliament. The monarch has the task of making sure the people are happy and at the same time giving support to the parliament and government like an elder sibling or a loving parent.

This model has been used for many years at Plum Village, and it has brought about much happiness for the Sangha. I have suggested this model to those building the Sangha at the newer centers as well.

The Caretaking Council

Every hamlet at Plum Village has a caretaking council. The caretaking council puts into effect the decisions made with the sanghakarman procedure described in Chapter 3 and cannot change these decisions without another meeting of the bhikshu or bhikshuni assembly. Sisters or brothers are invited onto the caretaking council because they have the abilities needed to care for the Sangha in matters of organization. The council includes novices as well as those who have received the bhikshu or bhikshuni precepts. They do not have to be advanced in years or senior members of the community. Laypeople can also be chosen for the council to represent other laypeople. The caretaking council represents all of us, and members are nominated and voted for by the Sangha for a specific term of office.

Sometimes the caretaking council of the monastery may still be inexperienced. Elder brothers and sisters may see this and try to take over the work of the caretaking council, but this is incorrect practice, not consistent with what is taught in the monastic discipline. The elders cannot do the work of the council, although they have the right to offer their opinion or give the caretaking council a helping hand. All the practice centers and hamlets of Plum Village follow this principle. We know that a caretaking council may not be very strong in the beginning, but with practice it will gradually gather experience and strength. We trust in the saying: "Teach me and I shall forget, show me and I shall remember, let me do it and I shall understand." There are younger brothers and sisters who in the beginning thought they could not contribute much, but later they became very skillful members of the Sangha. They thought: "Let the elders do the work. We are still very immature and we cannot undertake this important task." When we gave them the opportunity to take the tiller into their hands, they grew up very quickly and became good leaders.

Meetings of the caretaking council can be very simple. For example, the members may sit down together with a pot of tea and in a short time, with much joy and enthusiasm, decide what work needs to be done to prepare for a certain event. For example, the bhikshus and the novices of the Upper Hamlet often drink tea together and exchange their insights. Then when the time comes for a formal meeting, the final decision is reached easily. Once, when I heard someone criticizing these monks for drinking a little too much tea, I smiled and said: "If the monks drink tea mindfully and practice building brotherhood, it is sometimes more effective than long hours of sitting meditation or reciting the sutras without looking at each other." Any practice that helps resolve difficulties and establishes communication between members of the Sangha is very precious. Such practices can even make possible the "six togethernesses."[4]

The different caretaking councils at the hamlets of Plum Village do not all work in exactly the same way, and each council can learn many valuable lessons from the other councils. There is a Vietnamese saying: "If the elder sister falls, the younger sister helps her up." The caretaking councils of the different hamlets put the spirit of this saying into practice by offering each other mutual help and affection. This helps the work of our entire community to flow smoothly. An important principle of the caretaking council is the art of being flexible and not becoming caught in minor formalities. Just as an airplane's flight path is without the limits of a train's rails, the flexibility of the caretaking council is like the freedom of a bird flying in the vast blue sky.

The Abbot or Abbess

The abbot or abbess of every temple or hamlet is nominated by its permanent residents and assisted by the caretaking council. The role of the abbess is very important for the happiness of the Sangha. Her first duty is to look after all members of the Sangha, from the eldest to the youngest. Just like a mother or elder sister, when she sees that a younger sister in the Sangha is not very happy, she comes to her and asks how she is doing, comforting and supporting her. The abbess looks after the happiness of the Sangha by being present for every-one twenty-four hours each day.

The second responsibility of the abbot or the abbess is to find ways to develop the skills and abilities of every person in the Sangha. Everyone has a talent of one kind or another. Even though someone is not good at typing, she may sing well. Though he may not be able to make beautiful furniture, he may have a lot of experience in organization. When the abbot knows how to recognize the talents of his brothers and gives them the opportunity to realize their talents, it will make the Sangha as a whole very happy. There is no more beautiful task than spending one's time in this work of love, discov-ering the talents of everyone in the Sangha.

The abbot or abbess also has the duty to support the caretaking council and to contribute ideas and energy to the council while it is carrying out the decisions of the Sangha. When she sees a difficulty that needs to be resolved, she can take steps to help resolve it. However, she cannot take over the duties of the caretaking council nor do some-thing on behalf of the caretaking council. She allows the caretaking council to have its full responsibility. Sometimes the abbess may see that an important matter requires a meeting of the entire commu-nity, and she will be the one to assemble the meeting. Or, the abbess may suggest a simple way of resolving the matter. For example, if a sis-ter falls sick suddenly and needs to go to the hospital, the abbess as a representative of the Sangha can take responsibility for the decision.

The Dharmacharya Council

Another structure at Plum Village is the dharmacharya council. It includes monks and nuns who have received the "lamp transmis-sion" to become Dharma teachers. The dharmacharya council is responsible for training all the monastic and lay brothers and sisters in the practice. Dharmacharya must devote all their time and atten-tion to being a teacher. Teaching the Dharma is something that requires one's whole being. Every step and every breath becomes a

Dharma talk. Dharmacharya teach not only by words but also in the way they live their daily lives, in the way they speak with harmony and love, and in the way they walk with mindfulness. Dharmacharya become an example for their younger brothers and sisters and for everyone who comes to practice with them. They must help as many people as possible profit from the deep and wonderful teachings of the Buddha since so many people are thirsty to receive the Dharma.

Weekly Bhikshu and Bhikshuni Meetings

Recently I have encouraged the fully ordained members of the community to sit together once a week to ensure the happiness and harmony of the community. The meeting should not be longer than one hour so that we do not find it tiresome. The regularity of the meeting helps keep a steady connection and flow of communication between us. The bhikshus and bhikshunis form the core of the community. It is important that they are in harmony with one another and that they have an opportunity to discuss and take care of important matters together. We can share about concerns such as finances, ordinations, building projects, and so on. But the most important thing to discuss is the well-being and happiness of the sisters and brothers in our community.

The meeting should not only be for discussion. It should also be a light and nourishing time together. We can begin with a song or a poem that is inspiring to us and supports us in the practice. We can serve some tea. One sister or brother will be asked to facilitate the meeting. After a few moments enjoying our tea and being together, the facilitator may invite the sisters and brothers to begin sharing. Generally it is best to have a list beforehand of things which will be discussed so that we know we have enough time and that each topic is appropriate for the meeting.

If someone is not well in the Sangha, this is a good time to bring out his or her case and offer suggestions of how to help him or her. If there is a conflict in the community, even a small one, we can also bring this out and offer possible routes to finding reconciliation. During the meeting everyone should follow his or her breathing and speak only with calm and loving kindness. In this way everyone feels comfortable to express him or herself and look deeply together in the spirit of a spiritual family.

The decisions that are made are much less important than the effect of nourishing our sense of brotherhood and sisterhood. With this as a foundation we will easily find ways to support each other and to resolve difficulties and uneasiness within the Sangha. When we feel the warmth and togetherness of our sisters and brothers, whatever matters need to be taken care of will flow easily and naturally without struggles and conflict. Our brotherhood and sisterhood are truly the foundation of living together harmoniously as a Sangha body.

This practice is the most recent offering that I have made to the Sangha body in Plum Village, so it will take some time to develop. Most likely each hamlet will find a slightly different way of structuring the weekly meetings to fit the community and circumstances. The essential thing is to maintain open communication and to ensure the well-being and happiness of the Sangha body.

In parallel with the bhikshu and bhikshuni meetings, there are also the novice meetings and laypeople meetings. And the "intersharings" of each of these meetings in turn will foster and nourish mutual understanding and happiness.

In a family we can also have a weekly meeting. Sitting together like this we have an opportunity to discuss issues that are important for our happiness. If a son or daughter has a difficulty in school or the mother or father has a dilemma in the workplace, this can be presented and the whole family can offer their insight as to how to improve the situation. The family that practices is really like a Sangha, and a Sangha is just like a family, so it is natural if they function in similar ways. You don't have to call yourselves Buddhist to apply these practices into your life. They are simply a matter of bringing peace and joy to your family and your community.

In a workplace a weekly meeting is also important. In fact, many offices already have such a meeting. But it is the way in which we conduct the meeting that can determine whether it benefits our happiness or not. Please be creative with your meeting so that everyone feels included and nourished. When people have a sense of connection to each other they will be able to work together more joyfully and successfully. When we have a meeting like this we may find that the energy in the workplace goes up.

The following is the text of a meditation which we read before our Sangha meetings in Plum Village. You may like to write a similar text that is appropriate for your own community meetings in your Sangha, in your family or in your workplace:

Meditation before meetings

> Dear Lord Buddha and All Our Ancestral Teachers:
> We vow to go through this meeting in a spirit of togetherness as we review all ideas and consolidate them to reach a harmonious understanding or consensus. We vow to use the methods of loving speech and deep listening in order to bring about the success of this meeting as an offering to the Three Jewels. We vow not to hesitate to share our ideas and insights but also vow not to say anything when the feeling of irritation is present in us. We are resolutely determined not to allow tension to build up in this meeting. If any one of us senses the start of tension, we will stop immediately and practice Beginning Anew right away so as to re-establish an atmosphere of togetherness and harmony.

Encouraging the Young Members of the Sangha

Sometimes the younger members of a family or community have ways of looking at a situation that are more insightful than the point of view of their elders. We should encourage the younger members of the community to speak out, since sharing their insight, even if it is not in accord with what the majority or the elders are thinking, can contribute to the Sangha body. The eyes of one person, even one who has studied and practiced for a long time, are still only the eyes of one individual. But the eyes of the Sangha body are those that see widest and deepest. When the Sangha has a matter to resolve, it should rely on the Sangha eyes to look for a solution, never on the eyes of one individual alone.

Often younger members of the Sangha are afraid to say something that their elders may not agree with, or they may be inexperienced and shy about speaking in front of a large assembly. It is important for elders to be able to listen deeply to the younger generation and to encourage them by saying: "Younger brother, please tell us your idea. Maybe it is at variance with what the elder brothers think, but please do not hold back. To speak out is your duty as a member of the Sangha. Please be brave and contribute to the happiness of the Sangha by expressing your idea." This kind of encouragement is needed all the time to help the young ones speak out. It should be the daily practice of elder brothers and sisters in the Sangha.

Practicing like this leads to ease of communication and openness in the Sangha. It removes the heavy atmosphere that arises when people feel they cannot speak out. When we feel we can voice our ideas from our hearts, our minds no longer feel heavy and constricted. This makes the happiness of the Sangha grow quickly. After only one week of practice, the happiness of the Sangha can be doubled. When a young person has been able to express her idea to the Sangha, she feels that she is contributing to the running of the Sangha. As a result, she does not feel pulled along by the current or pushed out to the margin of Sangha life.

So many generations of parents, teachers, elder brothers, and sisters have considered the opinions of children to be unimportant. They feel that children do not have enough experience and that what they think or want does not matter. Elders may believe that they know what is best for the younger brothers and sisters. This is not

necessarily true. When elders have not yet fully understood or listened deeply to the difficulties and the deep wishes of their younger
brothers and sisters, they cannot truly love them. Love has to come
from understanding. When love is not based on understanding it is
harmful. Without being aware of it, parents commonly cause their
children to suffer, and elder brothers and sisters cause the younger
ones to suffer.

Novices are not only novices, and children are not only children.
They are always in the process of growing, and we need to allow them
the opportunity to mature. When we help novices or children grow
up, we have a future. In Plum Village in recent years we have been
very happy to see how quickly young monks and nuns develop new
skills. In the beginning no one would have imagined that these
monks and nuns could assume the position of a work coordinator or
an abbot. But since they have new insights and techniques they are
able to do things that the preceding generation could not, making the
monastery run more smoothly.

The older generation needs to see this clearly and to stop thinking
that the younger generation is too inexperienced to do anything successfully. In many temples, there are elders who think: If I am not
there, everything will go wrong. When elders think like this, there is
no hope for the future. If younger ones are not able to grow up, it is
our own fault. The elder generation has to train and support the
younger people so that little by little they learn to play the roles that
the elders are now playing and become able to replace them. If the
Buddha had not practiced like this, the Sangha would not have been
able to continue steadily without him after he entered nirvana.

When elders give guidance or a helping hand, they must know
how to use loving speech and not reprimand younger brothers and
sisters for their mistakes. In Plum Village we have found that using
harsh words is useless. The only skillful method is to show love and
support. The face of a younger sister who is looking a little sad is like
the sound of the mindfulness bell to awaken us. We should ask ourselves: What has happened to make my little sister's face so sad? We

should not dismiss the matter by saying: Everyone has their ups and downs just as the weather is sometimes sunny and sometimes rainy. The unhappy face of a younger sister announces the difficulties she is going through. We should approach the younger sister and ask her how she is, encouraging her to talk about her difficulties.

At first a novice may not want to confide in her elder sister because she is afraid she will make her elder sister angry if what she says is at odds with the way her elder sister sees things. For the same reasons children are afraid to confide in their parents. If the younger one keeps all her feelings to herself, they will become a knot inside that causes her to become ill-tempered and uncommunicative and makes everyone suffer. The elders have to be patient and open their hearts. They have to prove that they have the capacity to listen deeply so that the younger sister or brother has enough confidence to say what she or he really thinks. The elders who are not able to do this are not yet fully playing the role of an elder.

The sad expression on the face of our younger brother or child is also an opportunity for us to examine our behavior and any mistakes we have made. To make a younger member of our Sangha happy is to make ourselves happy. If our younger brother can smile, it is our success. If the children are happy, it is the success of the parents.

Practicing with the Triangle

In our daily activities as a Sangha, very often a relationship evolves into what we call the "triangle." This is something that puts the happiness of the Sangha at risk. The triangle is created when one person in the Sangha is suffering, irritated, and upset at a second person and goes to a third person to complain. The one who is irritated has not yet learned to transform her suffering, to open her heart, to listen deeply, or to practice the art of loving speech. She is not able to go directly to the person whom she thinks is the cause of her suffering and talk to him. So she complains to her friend about the one who has made her suffer, pouring out all her dislike for him. This triangle can be established anywhere, in any community. It can also happen in our own family. Part of Sangha building is to prevent these triangles from forming. We have to find a way to stop it from blooming while it is still only a bud.

When we suffer and are not able to deal with our suffering, we search for someone who will listen to us. This is natural. Sharing our difficulties with a friend can be very beneficial. When we find a person who listens deeply, we already feel less suffering. If we were not allowed to talk about our difficulties and express our painful feelings, they would become like knots inside us. But if our brother or sister takes our side and joins us in blaming the third person, even though we may feel better, we will be forming a triangle. If we complain to someone and he takes our side in this way, it does not necessarily help us to suffer less. When we water our seeds of anger and ignorance these seeds will not have the opportunity and the right conditions to be transformed. Therefore we have to look deeply when we feel a need to look for someone to complain to.

All of us have also at some time or other had a friend come to us to complain. When our friend came to us we may have made a mistake and agreed to speak unlovingly about a third brother or sister. Therefore, we must practice how not to form the triangle. We should not turn away from our suffering friend and say: "I am sorry, I cannot listen to you complaining." When someone who is suffering comes to you, please practice listening deeply with an open mind and compassion.

By listening deeply we will discover what is in the heart of our suffering friend. By not taking sides, we can also try to understand the person who helped cause our friend's suffering. In telling her story, our friend may distort the truth because of her wrong perceptions, and after having listened deeply we can help her to see more clearly so that she will suffer less. As we express our love for our sister, we can help her undo her wrong perceptions and remind her that the other person may have been unskillful in one way, but that he has many good qualities as well. When we do this skillfully, her heart will soften and she will suffer less. We can also suggest that our sister and brother meet together, with us there to help them find peace and joy, and to help restore the happiness of the Sangha.

Sometimes we may also find ourselves standing outside a triangle. Sooner or later the triangle will damage the happiness of our community or family, and we will suffer also. In these times, we can also practice Sangha building by talking with our brothers and sisters in the triangle. Or if we feel we are not able to practice by ourselves, we can call on someone else, perhaps our teacher or an elder who has more skill, and ask him or her to help in resolving the matter.

In any Sangha, lay or monastic, the triangle is a tiny shoot that sprouts from the seed of division and unhappiness in the community. If the shoot continues to grow, the community will become more unhappy. Everyone in the Sangha has the duty to uproot the triangle before it can grow. This is the work of Sangha building, and it has been used in Plum Village for many years now.

More Sangha-Building Practices

THE SECOND BODY

The second body system is a Sangha building practice at Plum Village. In a large Sangha, it isn't possible to be close to everyone, so we are each given a "second body" to take special care of. Your own body is your "first body," and a Dharma sister may be your second body. Her second body may be another sister, and so on. In this way, everyone has someone to look after, and everyone is looked after by someone else. "Looking after" means taking care of and helping our second body when she is physically ill, afflicted in mind, or overworked. For example, when you are traveling together, you are responsible to see that your second body is not left behind. When your second body's spirits are low, you can find a way to raise them. When your second body is not able to smile, you can help her to smile.

When he has the flu, you can bring him food and medicine. If you need to, you can also ask for the help of an elder brother, sister, or lay friend in the Sangha.

We use the second body practice in all the Plum Village practice centers, and it is something we take seriously. This practice raises the quality of our happiness living together. Many lay Sanghas also practice the second body system. It can be a wonderful way to stay connected to the whole Sangha by taking care of just one member of the Sangha. In a large family we could do the same.

THE MENTOR SYSTEM

Another practice we use is the mentor system. A mentor is someone who has practiced for some time. Because of his or her experience, he or she is a refuge for younger sisters and brothers for whom the practice is still something new. The Chinese word for mentor, *yi zhi shi*, means someone we can take refuge in. In French, the word for mentor, *tuteur*, refers to the stake we use to support a newly planted sapling. We put this stake into the earth next to the sapling so that the sapling can lean against it when it is weak. With the support and guidance of the stake the young tree is helped to grow upright and strong.

Someone who has practiced for many years, including a layperson, can be a mentor for several other practitioners. In the time of the Buddha, monks who were practicing well could be mentors for ten or twenty new practitioners, and there were even those who mentored thirty or forty. In our own time at Plum Village, the senior monks and nuns mentor generally from four to ten people. In families, parents are the mentors. Sometimes, in larger families, elder brothers or sisters can play the role of mentor for the younger siblings. The Chinese expression *di zi*, which is usually translated as "disciple," also means younger brother and son. This is a very good expression, because our younger Dharma brother is also like our son; our younger Dharma sister is also like our daughter. When we take care of them, we are taking care of ourselves.

The person who is being looked after is called a "mentee." A mentor takes responsibility for the quality of the mentee's practice and spiritual life and should understand what is happening in these areas. She does not have to be capable in every aspect of guiding and teaching a mentee. In Plum Village there are monks and nuns who have been practicing for only three or four years when they are appointed mentor for those who are newly ordained. They give very good guidance. If a mentor encounters difficulties she is not able to resolve on her own, she can also ask for the help of an elder brother or sister who has more experience in the practice or who is more at ease, peaceful, and joyful.

A mentor should also report to the dharmacharya council every month about the progress of his mentee so that the dharmacharya will know what teachings are needed in the Sangha. When a teacher gives a Dharma talk, he or she needs to know what is happening in the daily life of the Sangha to offer teachings that will be useful for the Sangha to put into practice.

Shining Light

Another method for Sangha building is the practice called "Shining Light" or "offering guidance". It is based on the traditional pavarana ceremony at the close of the rains retreat, in which the monastic Sangha looks deeply into the practice of each member to let that person know how they should practice in order to make progress. Based on the terms "Buddha eyes," "wisdom eyes," and "Dharma eyes" found in the sutras, we have invented the term "Sangha eyes." These are the collective eyes of the whole Sangha, which can see the truth more clearly and more deeply than the eyes of a single brother or sister and can shine light on the practice of each brother and sister.

The practice of Shining Light in Plum Village differs somewhat from the traditional pavarana, or invitation practice. In the traditional ceremony, each monk (or nun) comes before an elder brother and wholeheartedly invites him to describe the shortcomings he has observed in his younger brother during the course of the three-month rains retreat. In Plum Village we sincerely invite and request every brother or sister in our own hamlet—whether they are elder or younger—to shine light on us. They not only point out our short-comings but tell us first of all what we have excelled in. Then, they offer us concrete practices to maintain and increase our good qualities while transforming what is unwholesome. We also receive a letter that we can read to encourage us in our practice and to remind us of what we need to transform.

Before each session of Shining Light we read the following letter out loud for the entire Sangha to reflect upon and to help maintain at atmosphere of mutual respect and love.

> Dear Lord Buddha and all our Ancestral Teachers:
> Today we will shine light on the practice of our elder brothers or sisters and our younger brothers or sisters. We know that all of us are the various parts of one Sangha body and that we are the bones and flesh of the same Sangha body. Knowing this, we are aware that in shining light on the practice of any one member of the Sangha we are shining light on our own practice. We vow to do the practice of shining light with all our love and under-standing. We vow that everything we say will stem from the wholesome intention of reaching as accurate an insight as we can about our brother or sister and of offer-ing concrete suggestions of practice that will help our brother or sister in the process of true transformation. We vow to avoid allowing our anger and misperceptions dis-tort our views. We vow that every word spoken will be from a place of love within us.
>
> We know that in shining light on a member of the Sangha, we are also shining light on our own being. Thus, the practice of Shining Light will also be very beneficial for each and every one of us. We ask Lord Buddha and all our

spiritual ancestors to protect and support us so that this
Shining Light session will be a great success.

Sangha members should not take advantage of the Shining Light
practice to criticize and condemn each other. It is very important
that everything we say about a brother or sister comes from a heart
of love. If there is any anger or irritation in us, it is better not to
speak. We are shining light on our brother because we want him to
realize the highest fruits of the practice.

In the process of shining light we combine our ideas and insights.
In the process of listening to others' sharing we may modify our own
ideas. Listening to our sisters and brothers share about the one
receiving the shining light may help us to release our wrong perceptions about that person. Our insights are also stimulated by listening
to others speak. These are important benefits of the shining light.
While listening, we learn more about the reality of our brothers and
sisters and also about our own reality, thus having an opportunity to
understand ourselves more deeply. Usually we are able to recognize
that the strengths and the shortcomings of the other person can also
be found in ourselves. In this process we can reflect deeply and allow
ourselves to be transformed.

The art of shining light can be applied to nonsectarian groups as
well. When we sit together in this way we combine our ideas and
insights, and we arrive at a collective insight.

THE ART OF WATERING FLOWERS

I still remember a year when many families came to Plum Village
from Toulouse and Bordeaux to participate in a celebration of the
Buddha's birthday. In my Dharma talk that day I spoke about the art
of watering flowers as a Buddhist practice. "Watering flowers" means
giving encouragement by showing someone who is close to us their
good qualities and our appreciation of those qualities. As I spoke,
the eyes of a lady in the audience became full of tears. After the walking meditation that day, I came near to her husband and said: "My

friend, your flower needs some water." He listened to what I had to say, and on his way home to Bordeaux he practiced the art of watering flowers. By the time they arrived his wife had become a new person. She had so much more happiness than before.

The husband had often heard teachings about the art of watering flowers in order to make yourself and others happy, but he had not practiced it. For a long time he had failed to see what a precious jewel he had in his wife. He was like the son in the *Lotus Sutra* whose father sewed a precious jewel into the hem of his son's coat. The son was unaware of its presence and wandered everywhere in search of riches. It is always beneficial to remind our loved ones of our appreciation for them. They are precious treasures that will not always be with us. Please practice watering the flowers of your beloved ones. They, together with your brothers and sisters in the Sangha, may need your words of appreciation and encouragement. The practice of watering flowers is an expression of our gratitude. When we are grateful we will no longer suffer so much.

Beginning Anew

In the tradition of monastic life there is also the practice of repentance. When a monk or nun has made a mistake he or she comes before the Sangha body, prostrates, and kneels down to express her sincere regret. She shares her mistake and asks for the compassion and support of her fellow practitioners to improve her practice in the future.

In Plum Village, in addition to this traditional form of repentance, we have created an updated way of practicing. We also call this the practice of "Beginning Anew." We begin with flower watering as described in the last section. After we have recognized and acknowledged the beautiful and wholesome qualities in the other person, we may either share our regret for our unskillfulness and mistake or a hurt that we have felt from our sister or brother's unskillfulness. We may be in the presence of the whole community or with just a few practitioners present to support us. We practice speaking calmly and gently. We practicing listening deeply and openly without judging or discriminating against what we hear. In this way the process of reconciliation can happen.

We should not underestimate the first step of flower watering. When we can sincerely recognize the beautiful qualities of other people, it is very difficult to hold onto our feelings of anger and resentment. We will naturally soften and our perspective will become wider and more inclusive of the whole reality. When we are no longer caught in misperceptions, irritation, and judgment, we can easily find the way to reconcile ourselves with others in our community or family. The essence of this practice is to restore love and understanding between members of the community. The form that the practice takes needs to be appropriate to the situation and people involved. It is always helpful to consult with others who have more experience in the practice and have gone through similar difficulties in order to benefit from their experiences.

Bringing Our Teacher Inside

One morning as I was about to open the door and walk outside, the door opened suddenly from the other side. I met a monk who was in such a hurry that he opened the door without mindfulness. As he opened it he saw me standing inside. Such a monk or nun may say to others, "Oh, but usually I walk very mindfully and open the door very mindfully. Today I happened to be forgetful for the first time." Because I knew how the monk was feeling, I did not want to blame him. I just smiled gently. To me, the fact that he was aware of his lack of mindfulness was enough.

Let us not be caught in outer appearances and wait for our teacher to be there in the flesh in order to feel him alongside us. I had been taught by my own teacher when I was sixteen years old how to open a door with ease and mindfulness. Now, my teacher is in me all the time because he has transmitted himself to me. Your teacher is in you because he has transmitted himself to you. Your teacher is in every cell of your body already. Whenever you walk or stand in mindfulness, your teacher is walking and standing with you. In one of my poems it says: "My child, on your way home let your steps be in freedom." That is the practice of doing as you have seen your teacher do.

If you look deeply, you will see that the true way to have a really deep relationship with your teacher is to take steps in mindfulness just as your teacher does. When you step like that, the energy of your teacher will be powerful and will overflow in you. You will see that you and your teacher are one. You do not need to take many steps; you need only to take one step with all the ease and freedom possible. That step will take you back to your teacher, and you will see that you are truly close to him. You do not necessarily have to wait for your teacher to arrive in person in order to be close to him.

In the *Vajracchedika Sutra,* The *Diamond That Cuts through Illusion,*[5] the Buddha taught: "If you look for me in form, then you are not practicing the right path and you will not be able to see the Tathagata." We can translate these words again by saying: "If you look for me *only* in form . . . . " We add the word "only" to make it clearer. You may ask: "Well, why can't we discover the Buddha through the outer form? How can you say that the thirty-two auspicious marks and the eighty minor marks, the name 'Siddhartha', and the person sitting on the Vulture Peak are not really the Buddha?" You are partly right, but the meaning in the sutra is that the Buddha is not *only* his body. If you look for Buddha only in his physical form, then you will be caught in the form, caught in appearance. If you know how to look for Buddha in things that are not his physical form, then you will not be caught in the form.

It is the same with your own teacher. Whenever you take a step with mindfulness, happiness, and as a free person, you see that your teacher is present in you in that moment. When you come across a brother or sister who is going along in a rush, you know that they do not have their teacher in them. There are people among us who from time to time, because of the work they are doing, become hurried and forgetful, and they are not able to return to their breathing or maintain mindful steps. You can remind them by just lifting up your finger and smiling. This is how you bring back the true face of the teacher to that person. Even if you are a younger sister or brother, you can do this to help your elder brother or sister.

We have the duty to help each other, because no one is perfect in the practice of mindfulness. Do not say that the other person is not practicing. The other person does practice, but their practice has just not reached the highest level. We are the same. We may not yet have reached the level we would like in our practice. So as brothers and sisters, let us help each other in a kind way, without condemning or blaming. We need to be with the Buddha, our teacher, in every moment of our daily life, and then our happiness and our peace will grow.

❦ CHAPTER 6
Nourishing Our Families

THE PROBLEMS we encounter in a monastic Sangha are also problems that can arise in a family, whether the family is practicing a spiritual path or not. To bring happiness to the family, you can bring the practices of monastic life to the home life. If a family practices mindfulness, then they will know how to deal with problems and will be able to avoid the storms of disharmony. If members of the family do not practice, the family will become unhappy, and they will have no joy left.

The life of the Sangha can be a model so that families can also live together joyfully. For example, we can look on our father as an abbot and our mother as an abbess. Fathers and mothers should allow their children to participate in making decisions which relate to the happiness of the whole family. This will make everyone's life in the family happy and help the children grow into adulthood quickly and easily.

In a family, even if it is as small as two people, the family life can be organized democratically. Parents should not think that their children, because they are still young, are unintelligent. Children have good ideas and the wish to share them. It is very important for the happiness of the family that parents know how to listen deeply to their children. When you know how to listen deeply to your children and accept the value of their opinions, your children will know how to listen deeply to you and to understand you better also.

The Triangle in the Family

The "triangle" described in Chapter 5 also happens quite often in a family. Our children are still very innocent. When they hear mother talking about the bad habits and the unfortunate ways of their father, they believe that everything she says is true. The children become the victims of their mother's suffering. They suffer with their mother because they have doubts about their father and because they see that their mother and father are not happy together. The worst happens when the children take their mother's side against their father. Perhaps the father does make mistakes, but he needs understanding and compassion more than condemnation. It is not difficult for a parent to entice a little child to take her side because children do not yet have an independent point of view. If your child loves you and you encourage him to dislike the other parent, you are misusing your child's love for you, and everyone will suffer.

Once the family is caught in the triangle, happiness vanishes—whether that triangle has been formed by the father or the mother. This situation can carry on for many months or even years. Eventually it can cause the family to break, which is both painful and damaging. The key to bringing happiness back to the family is the presence of a Sangha. If the family practices with a local Sangha, the mother, father, or children can call on the Sangha for help. The eyes of the Sangha will see how the triangle is forming, and they will help you break it as a way of supporting your happiness. When friends come to visit, they can talk to the children about the positive points of their father, and the children will be able to see their father more clearly. Sangha friends will also see that although mother is very kind, there are also times when she is unskillful in the way she treats their father. They can say: "Children, you should help your mother to treat your father more gently and to be more joyful in his presence." Children have more than enough ability to do this. With the help of the Sangha, they can bring joy back to the family.

When Parents Quarrel

It is easy to make young girls and boys happy. But one thing children are really afraid of is the quarreling of their parents. When parents lose their temper and make each other suffer, the children suffer most of all. When parents fight they often seem to forget that their children are with them in the house, and they do not see the suffering of the children. Adults have a thicker skin and are able to bear the suffering more easily than their children. The hearts of young children are still very open, and whenever they see their father and their mother shouting at each other, it is heartbreaking for them.

Sometimes children have to run and find a place to hide from their parents. In past times when people lived in the countryside, there was always a garden with apple trees, orange trees, or a pond surrounding the house. The children had a place to escape the suffocating atmosphere by playing games and chasing butterflies or dragonflies. The children could also take refuge in a neighbor's house and play there with their friends. Today we do not have such an environment. Most families live in towns with large apartment buildings or unsafe streets. When father and mother are angry at each other, the children do not have a place to run away to. Many of them have to go into the bathroom or bedroom to cry on their own.

The wounds children receive in this way are serious and may take many years to heal. Children will carry these wounds in their hearts even when they have grown up. There are many children who tell themselves they will not marry and have children of their own because they have suffered from their parents fighting with each other. There are children only seven or eight years old who have already made this decision. Parents should do their best to stop this misfortune befalling their children. Parents should not allow themselves to quarrel in front of the children. Whenever the atmosphere in the family becomes heavy, like the dark clouds before a storm, parents should find ways to let the storm to pass over quickly so that it does not linger in the house for a long time.

The Breathing Room

In Plum Village we offer the practice of the breathing room. Every house should have a room called the breathing room, or at least a corner of a room reserved for this purpose. In this place you can put a low table with a flower, a little bell, and enough cushions for everyone in the family to sit on. When you feel uneasy, sad, or angry, you can go into this room, close the door, sit down, invite a sound of the bell, and practice breathing mindfully. When you have breathed like this for ten or fifteen minutes, you begin to feel better. If you do not practice like this, you can lose your temper. Then you may shout or pick a fight with the other person, creating a huge storm in your family.

On one summer retreat at Plum Village, I asked a young boy, "My child, when your father speaks in anger, do you have any way to help your father?" The child shook his head: "I do not know what to do. I become very scared and try to run away." When children come to Plum Village they can learn about the breathing room so they can help their parents when they become angry. I told the young boy, "You can invite your mother or father into your breathing room to breathe with you."

This is something the family must agree on in advance. When everyone is feeling happy, this is a good occasion to ask your father and mother to sign an agreement. You could say: "Daddy, Mommy, sometimes you are angry with each other and say things to hurt each other. This makes me very afraid. Next time this happens, am I allowed to go into the breathing room and invite the sound of the bell to remind you to breathe as our teacher in Plum Village has taught us?" If, at that particular moment, father and mother are feeling happy, they will both be very eager to agree. "Of course, my child, next time you see that we are not agreeing, you have the right to go into the breathing room and invite the bell. This will help us remember to breathe together so that we will not make the whole family suffer."

As young children, you are still very fresh. You can use your freshness to help your parents. You can say to your mother: "Mommy, whenever father says something out of anger which hurts you, you could follow me into the breathing room and we could breathe together instead of arguing with Daddy. What do you think?" If your mother agrees with you, then when your father says something unkind, you go to your mother and take her hand, saying to her: "Let's go into the breathing room, Mommy." When father sees this it will wake him up. He will feel admiration for his wife and child because they know how to practice in difficult moments. You can do the same with your father. Whenever mother says something unkind to upset father so that he is about to lose his temper, you can come and take your father's hand, saying quietly: "Daddy, don't be upset. Let's both go into the breathing room."

Once you have gone into the breathing room, you have the sound of the bell and the Buddha to protect you. Everyone in the family can sign an agreement which states: "When we hear the sound of the bell in the breathing room, it is the sound of the Buddha calling us, and everyone in the house will stop and breathe. No one will continue to shout after that." The whole family can make this commitment to stop and breathe at the sound of the bell. This is called "the agreement on living together in peace and joy," which we propose to every family that comes to Plum Village. If you can bring this method of practice home, after about three months you will feel that the atmosphere in the family has become much more pleasant. The wounds in the hearts of the children will be soothed, and gradually they will heal.

The Cake That Is Always Replenished

If you have not yet been able to buy a bell or set up a breathing room at your home, you can use a cake. It is a very special cake that I transmit to the children who come to Plum Village so that they can take it home and practice with it. This cake is not made of flour and sugar like a sponge cake. You can keep eating it, and it is never finished. It is called "the cake in the refrigerator."

There will come a day when you are sitting in the living room or dining room and you see that your mother and father are about to lose their temper with each other. As soon as the atmosphere becomes heavy and unpleasant, you can use the practice of the cake to restore harmony in your family. First of all, breathe in and out three times to give yourself enough courage, and then look at your mother and say to her: "Mommy, Mommy." Your mother will look at you and ask: "What is it, my child?" And you will say: "I remember that we have a cake in the refrigerator." Whether or not there is really a cake in the refrigerator does not matter. The reason you say this is to help your mother avoid quarreling with your father.

Saying "there is a cake in the refrigerator" really means: "Daddy, Mommy, don't make each other suffer anymore." When they hear these words, your parents will understand. Your mother will look at you and will say: "Quite right! My child, will you go out on the veranda and arrange the table and the chairs while I go and fetch the cake and the tea." When mother says this, you have already found a way out of the dangerous situation. You can run out on to the veranda and wait for her. Your mother now has an opportunity to withdraw from the fight with your father. Before you spoke up, she could not stand up and leave since it would be very impolite and it might pour more oil onto the flames of your father's anger. Now, she can go into the kitchen. As she opens the refrigerator to take out the cake and boils the water to make the tea, she can follow her breathing as she learned in Plum Village. If there is no real cake in the refrigerator, don't worry. Your mother is talented and she will find something to substitute for the cake. As she prepares the cake and tea she can smile the half smile to feel lighter in body and spirit.

While father is sitting alone in the living room, he will recognize that his wife and child are practicing what they learned in Plum Village. He will think to himself: "If I don't practice, then it will look very strange. It will look as if I don't remember what we all learned together." He will also begin to practice breathing in mindfulness. Gradually his hot temper will calm down, and he will begin to feel affection for his wife and child. After the tea and the cake have been placed on the table, he may walk out slowly onto the veranda to join the tea party with his wife and child in an atmosphere that is light and full of understanding. If your father is hesitant to come out, then you can run into the house, take your father's hand, hold it to your cheek, and coax him by saying: "Daddy, do you love me? Daddy, come and have some tea and cake with me."

Please take this practice home with you. You will be bringing Plum Village back to your home, and life in the family will become peaceful.

The Priceless Inheritance

Parents always want their children to have happiness in the future, and that is why they think about leaving things like a house, a piece of land, or a savings account to their children. Parents also want to help give their children an education so they will be happy with a career in medicine, engineering, or some other field. The parents' love expresses itself in their desire for their children to have a firm foundation for a secure future.

It is only natural that parents should have wishes like this, but this way of showing love is not the sort of love that children need most of all. Generally, children do not need as much material security as the parents think. What children need most of all is a peaceful life in the family. When the parents are living together in harmony, children have happiness right away and they also have the foundation for happiness in the future. Young people who come to Plum Village all agree that the most precious gift parents can offer their children is their own happiness.

What is more important, however, is that when the children grow up and find partners, they will also be able to bring happiness to their own families. While they were living with their parents, they saw how their mother and father looked after each other. They heard their father say gracious things to their mother, and they heard their mother say gentle things to their father. Father and mother made each other happy by the way they spoke and acted. Although the parents were not directly teaching their children in words, they were teaching their children by the way they behaved towards each other. This is the most effective way of teaching. In Buddhism it is called "teaching by means of our person." Thanks to this, the children will be able to do as their parents have done.

The family is a university in which the two most important professors are the father and mother. If father and mother can understand each other, love each other, and make each other happy, they will create a wonderful atmosphere for their children to be born into and grow up in. When they graduate from this university, the children will have the capacity to make those they love happy. Father and mother should remember that in the family they do not only play the role of father and mother, but they also play the role of professors, teaching the lesson of love to their children.

Whenever a father makes a mistake that causes his wife to suffer, he should know how to apologize. After the evening meal the father could invite his wife and child into the breathing room, invite three sounds of the bell, and then say: "I'm sorry Mother, I'm sorry my child. I was very angry this morning, and because I lacked mindfulness, I said something unkind to Mother. I promise that I will practice not speaking angry words to Mother anymore." Once he has spoken like this the whole family should become silent, following their breathing in order to absorb the feeling of love in the room. This love has come about because you have known how to practice the teachings of mindfulness. After that father invites three sounds of the bell, the whole family stands up, and they all hug each other before leaving the breathing room. No one needs to say anything more.

If the father can speak like this to mother, the children will have great admiration and respect for their father. If the mother has the capacity to forgive, to be tolerant, and to hug father, then the children will have great admiration and respect for mother. They will see that their father and mother are ideal models for them in life. But if father uses his authority to yell at his children and does not allow them to speak, the children will not have any admiration for him. You can only learn from the people you admire. The true authority of father and mother lies in the fact that they know how to respect each other and make each other happy.

The Buddha teaches us about the cycle of birth and death, *samsara*. This is a cycle in which the same suffering repeats itself. If we do not practice, we will not be able to step out of it. Your grandmother may have had unwholesome habit energies such as anger or depression that she handed on to your mother. Your mother may then hand these habit energies on to you, and you can hand them on to your own children. This is called samsara. It is a vicious cycle, but the practice can transform it. If you practice mindfulness, you will not hand on these negative things to your children and grandchildren in the future. Practicing mindfulness is the only way to put an end to the vicious cycles that have been passed down for so many generations. We can transform the negative habit energies we have received from our father and mother and not hand them on to our children in the future. This is the deepest way of showing our gratitude to our ancestors.

Looking Deeply in the Family

One year there was a gentleman staying in the Upper Hamlet of Plum Village for several months. During that season I asked all residents of Plum Village, monastic and lay, to do the following exercise as a means of looking deeply into their blood family. I suggested that each person find a quiet place to sit, such as under a tree or in their room, and write down all the positive qualities of their mother and father. This gentleman began the exercise. First he wrote down all the beautiful qualities that he observed in his father. He thought: "Oh, it is easy to find good qualities in my father, but not in my mother." He had had many difficulties with his mother, and he couldn't imagine that she had any or many positive attributes. Still, he persevered with the exercise and tried to write down what he saw was positive in his mother.

He was quite surprised to find that the list for his mother eventually grew long. He had thought that there were no good qualities in his mother, but when he looked deeply he saw many beautiful things in himself that he knew didn't come from his father's side. He realized that those good qualities must come from his mother. In this way, his practice of looking deeply into his own self allowed him to see the beautiful things that he had received from his mother.

After recognizing the many good things about his mother, the gentleman decided to write a love letter to his mother. His love and respect for his mother had been restored, and he wished to share this directly with her. He wrote to his mother describing the beautiful qualities he had recognized in her and had received from her. Sometime later his wife phoned him at Plum Village and reported that his mother was very happy to receive his letter. After reading her son's letter she was so moved that she wished to write a similar letter to her own mother. Unfortunately, her own mother had already passed away. The gentleman told his mother, "You can still write to your mother because she is still alive in you. While you write the letter she will receive it."

It is a great offering we can make to ourselves, our beloved ones, and our ancestors to do the work of reconciliation. We reconcile with our mother and father inside of us, and we can also discover a skillful way to reconcile with our mother and father outside of us. It is never too late to bring peace and healing into our blood family.

Knowing How to Love

As a mother or father we may have the feeling that parents have much wisdom and experience, while children are still young and know very little. We may force our children to do what we think is best for them, and then the communication between us and our children will break down. When there is no more communication between us, how can we be happy? The most important thing is to keep communication alive between parents and children. When the door of communication has been shut, both parents and children suffer. But when we practice good communication, parents and children will share their lives together as friends, and that is the only way to find true happiness.

Buddhism teaches us how to use loving speech and how to listen deeply as two wonderful methods to open the door of communication. As parents we should not use the language of authority but the language of love when we speak to our children. When we can speak with the language of love and understanding, our children will come to us and will tell us about their difficulties, suffering, and anxieties. With this kind of communication we will understand our children, and only then can we really love them. Before that, we thought that we loved our children, but our love was not based on understanding. For the more we loved, the more our children felt stifled and miserable.

In Plum Village we often say that to love without knowing how to love, wounds the person we love. The person we love may be our son, our daughter, our wife, or our husband. To truly love, the father can say to the child: "My son, do you think that I understand you? Do you think that I understand your difficulties and your suffering? Please tell me. I want to know so that I can love you in such a way that does not hurt you." When a father says this, his son will have an opportunity to open his heart to the father. The same is true for a mother. A mother has to ask her daughter, "Darling, please tell me the truth. Do you think that I understand you? Do I understand your suffering, your difficulties, and your deepest wishes? If I do not yet understand, then please help me to understand. Because if I do not understand, I will continue to make you suffer in the name of love." This is what we call loving speech.

When our child is talking, please practice listening deeply. Sometimes our child will say something that surprises us. It is the opposite from the way we see things. All the same, we have to listen deeply. We should not be annoyed with her, because we have vowed to listen deeply to our children. Please allow your child to speak freely. Do not cut her off as she is talking or criticize what she says. When we listen deeply with all our heart—for half an hour, one hour, or even three hours—we will begin to see her more deeply. We will begin to understand her more, and we will begin to realize that although our child is still very small, she has some deep insights and her own special needs. We may also begin to realize that for a long time we have been making our child suffer. Parents have to look deeply at their children. Are they happy or are they suffering? If they are suffering, then we will suffer too.

Harmonizing Two Cultures

Today we live among people from many different cultures. We must practice the art of living joyfully together and learn to look deeply at each other's many beautiful qualities. We should have faith in our own culture, but we should also respect the customs of other societies. I used to offer this teaching to the many Vietnamese families I visit in North America and Europe, but it is also something very important to be learned by people in all cultures.

I meet many children of Vietnamese parents who are educated and grow up in a Western environment. They go to elementary school, high school, and university in the West, and they learn how to think, speak, and behave in a Western way. Maybe at school and in society the children have come into contact with aspects of Western culture that are not very wholesome or beautiful. This makes the parents feel uncomfortable when their children are acting or speaking in a Western way. The parents are often unhappy and criticize the way their children are behaving.

To blame the children like this is unjust. It can be confusing to the children. They do not understand why their parents are blaming them for speaking like an American and not having the manners of a Vietnamese person. They have been taught Western culture at school, and when they apply the customs of this culture at home they are criticized. Parents have to be fair when making this judgment. The education, guidance, and direction of your children is also your responsibility.

All cultures are very beautiful in some aspects. Sometimes parents come from a different culture than the culture that they live and raise their children in. In this case parents have to put the beautiful aspects of their native culture into practice in their own lives. Only then will they be able to find a way to pass their culture on to their children so that they too can apply in their own lives what is good and beautiful in their native culture.

The difficulty is that the parents are often too busy making money in order to buy several cars and a large house. They do not have time to spend with their children. They do not put enough energy into speaking gently and kindly to their children. When the parents are not able to express in their daily life the beautiful and good things of their native culture, how can they hope to pass them on to their children? If parents want the children to be able to preserve what is beautiful and good in their native culture, they have to open up the door of communication between themselves and their children.

Children of all cultural origins can also practice to renew their relationship with their parents. We can learn about the beautiful aspects of our parents' culture that we may not know about. We can make a cup of tea to offer our parents when they come home. We can sit down with them and tell them what has happened in school that day. We can ask them to tell us stories about their youth, their difficulties, and their happiness. If one weekend we spend time going to visit friends, we can spend the next weekend with our parents. Spending time with our parents and grandparents is nourishing and healing. When we learn how to treat our parents with respect and love, the whole family will be happy and joyful. When difficult situations arise we will know how to face them together and we will be able to support each other with skillfulness and love.

Jewels for Family Relations in Vietnamese Culture

Any culture, whether Western or Eastern, has both precious jewels and unhealthy elements. Wherever there are positive attributes, there will always be negative attributes. We need to practice diligently to keep renewing what is positive in our culture. We need to persevere in learning about and bringing into our lives the jewels that the cultures around us have to offer.

I always remind young people living in Europe and North America that there are so many beautiful aspects of Vietnamese culture. I like to share some of the ways that young people and adults in Vietnam relate with each other. In Vietnam, if you want to talk to your father or mother, you always begin with the word *thua,* meaning "respectfully to." For example, "respectfully to my father" or "respectfully to my mother." If you give something to an adult—like a cup of tea or a bowl of rice—you always do this with two hands. At the dining table the children never begin to eat before their parents, and before they begin to eat they say: "Mother, Father, please be invited to this meal."

Children can present any matter to their parents, but they can never contradict their parents. Contradicting and disputing are very different from discussing something. The difference comes in the way you use words and in your tone of your voice. When you are going out, you normally say: "Respectfully to my father (or mother), I am going out to play (or I am going to school or I am going to work.)" As soon as you come home, you also say: "Respectfully to my father or mother, I have just come home."

When your parents invite guests to the house, the children should present themselves to greet them: "Respected uncle who has just come," or "Greetings, uncle." Once you have greeted the guests you can help your father or mother to pour tea and then ask permission to go to your room. You should be invited first before you remain with the guests to talk to them. If you want to bring friends home to play, you should generally ask the permission of your parents first.

When your friends come to the house you should bring them to your parents to introduce them before you do anything else with them.

There are so many other beautiful Vietnamese traditions and practices, but if Vietnamese children can do just what is mentioned above, they will be considered very polite and deserve to be called the loyal children of their parents and good disciples of their teacher.

All the practices I have described in this chapter are things the whole family can practice together, creating moments of happiness that will nourish both the children and the parents. Mindfulness, concentration, and insight are the tools we are offered to renew ourselves, our relationships, and our communities. We can develop these qualities with all the concrete practices offered in this book.

Whether practicing together as a family, a Sangha, or a nation, we have so many opportunities to grow in our capacity to understand and to love. Each moment and each day is an opportunity to begin anew, to open the door of our hearts, and to practice together for our own transformation and healing and for the transformation and healing of our families and our world. Practicing together in this way we are discovering the path of living peacefully in the present moment and living joyfully together.

Notes

Notes to Chapter 1

1 "Upadhyaya" is a title for the senior monastic preceptor at an ordination ceremony for bhikshus and bhikshunis.

2 We do not see temporary exclusion from the Sangha as a punishment. It is a practice to give a monk or nun the space and time to look deeply in order to see more clearly where they are going. This monk or nun is asked to write a report to the Sangha to share with us the insights they have had while looking deeply. The practice of repentance means bowing before the Sangha, confessing our mistake and making the determination not to act in that way again.

3 Mindful manners help us to practice mindfulness in all our actions of body, speech, and mind and help us to live harmoniously together as a Sangha body. Novices at Plum Village study thirty-nine chapters of mindful manners, which offer detailed guidance for practicing mindfulness in such daily activities as attending our teacher, driving the car, cooking, and so on. They entail the basic training for monastics upon entering the monastery and the foundation for continuous practice of mindfulness throughout our lives as practitioners. See Thich Nhat Hanh, *Stepping into Freedom* (Berkeley: Parallax Press, 1997).

Notes to Chapter 2

1 For more information, see Thich Nhat Hanh, *Transformation at the Base* (Berkeley: Parallax Press, 2001).

2 See Thich Nhat Hanh, *Plum Village Chanting and Recitation Book* (Berkeley: Parallax Press, 2000) to find these recitations.

3 See Chapter 3. We are very fortunate to have both of these original versions of the sutra. Their content is about ninety percent the same, which means that what Venerable Maudgalyayana taught has been retained with little change. The differences between the two sutras are in the less important details, not in the essential content of the sutra.

4 Also called an "internal formation." The Sanskrit word is *samyojana* and the

Chinese *nei shi* or *jie shi*. It is a formation in our unconscious mind that binds us to a certain way of behavior in our daily life, causing us and the people around us to suffer.

5 For a detailed description of the practice of "Beginning Anew," see Chapter 5.

6 For a detailed description of the practice of "Shining Light," see Chapter 5.

Notes to Chapter 3

1 The Venerable Kassapa was generally respected in the Sangha as the fourth of the great disciples of the Buddha, coming after the Venerables Kondañña, Sariputra, and Maudgalyayana.

2 In Plum Village, we like to speak about "mindfulness trainings" rather than precepts. This is because we see that the precepts are a training in mindfulness. They are not an absolute right or wrong, but rather a direction that we go in. They are like the North Star that we use as a guiding light to take us in the direction of understanding, love, and compassion. Also the word "precepts" can have a heavy connotation for those from a Christian background who might feel that they are imposed on them from the outside. In reality, when we practice more deeply with them, we find that the mindfulness trainings are really a product of our own experience and insight gained from practicing mindfulness in our daily life.

3 Literally, "The Basket of Teachings Given on Discipline." The *Vinaya Pitaka* as we have it now has been added to since the time it was recited by the Venerable Upali at the First Council.

4 The three baskets, or *pitakas*, of the Buddha's teachings include the discourses delivered by the Buddha, *Sutta Pitaka*; the mindfulness trainings that determine the way of life of the Sangha, *Vinaya Pitaka*; and the writings that systematize and comment on the teachings of the Buddha, *Abhidhamma Pitaka*, or shastra.

5 There are two main transmissions of the teachings of the Buddha, the Northern and the Southern. The Southern based itself in Sri Lanka and the Northern in Kashmir.

6 The *pavarana*, or invitation, ceremony is continued in Plum Village under the name "Shining Light." See Chapter 5.

7 This *Vinaya Pitaka* is followed by monks and nuns in China, Vietnam, and all monasteries in Europe and America founded by Vietnamese or Chinese masters.

8 The Preceptor is the one who transmits the precepts during a precept transmission ceremony, whether it is for the five mindfulness trainings, the four-

teen mindfulness trainings, the novice precepts or the full precepts of a bhikshu or bhikshuni.

9 See Thich Nhat Hanh, *Our Appointment with Life* (Berkeley: Parallax Press, 1990) for complete text and commentary on the *Sutra on Knowing the Better Way to Live Alone.*

NOTES TO CHAPTER 4

1 For a detailed explanation of the practice of "Beginning Anew," see Chapter 5.

NOTES TO CHAPTER 5

1 Its full name is Tu Hieu Temple Named by Imperial Order. *Tu* means "loving kindness" and *Hieu* means "filial piety." Tu Hieu Temple is located on Duong Xuan hill in the Huong Thuy district of Thua Thien province. It was established by Zen Master Hai Thieu Cuong Ky, a disciple of the first patriarch of the school, Zen Master Nhat Dinh. In 1848, Master Hai Thieu Cuong Ky, along with the eunuchs of the palace in Hue, rebuilt the Nourished by Peace Hermitage and made it into a large temple. They did this in order to express their admiration for the practice of the first patriarch, Nhat Dinh, who was renowned for his qualities of loving kindness and compassion, his faithfulness to his parents, and his deep aspiration to help all beings. King Duc Tong, also known as Tu Duc, named this temple Tu Hieu in order to praise the love, compassion, and deep faithfulness of the first patriarch toward his parents. From then on, the temple has carried the name Tu Hieu Temple Named by Imperial Order.

2 This school was founded by Master Lin Chi in the ninth century in China. Teachers of this school came to Vietnam in two waves, first in the thirteenth century and again in the eighteenth.

3 This lineage began in central Vietnam in the eighteenth century as a new branch of the Lin Chi school.

4 *Saraniya-dhamma* in Pali and *liu he* in Chinese. These are six ways taught by the Buddha to maintain harmony in the Sangha: 1) harmony of the body by living together, 2) harmony of speech, which avoids disputes, 3) harmony of sharing, so that everyone benefits, 4) harmony of the precepts, which everyone practices together, 5) harmony of ideas, which brings joy, and 6) harmony of views, which leads to collective insight.

5 See Thich Nhat Hanh, *The Diamond That Cuts Through Illusion* (Berkeley: Parallax Press, 1992).